IMAGES OF ENGLAND

ASHINGTON
AND ITS MINING
COMMUNITY

ASHINGTON'S FOOTBALL HEROES

25 May - 14 July 1996

Woodhorn Colliery Museum
QE II Country Park
Ashington, Northumberland
Tel: (01670) 856968

Open: - Wednesday - Sunday
(and Bank Holiday Monday)
10am-5pm

- **Free Admission**
- **Free Car Parking**
- **Easy access from A189 coastal route**

Wor Jackie
Jack Charlton
Bobby Charlton
Jimmy Adamson
and over 80 other
footballing heroes

Includes memorabilia from the 1966 World Cup and many more rare photographs and momentos.

IMAGES OF ENGLAND

ASHINGTON
AND ITS MINING
COMMUNITY

MIKE KIRKUP

Frontispiece: Ashington's Football Heroes poster.

First published in 2004 by Tempus Publishing

Reprinted in 2008 by
The History Press
The Mill, Brimscombe Port,
Stroud, Gloucestershire, GL5 2QG
www.thehistorypress.co.uk

Reprinted in 2011, 2012

British Library Cataloguing in Publication Data.
A catalogue record for this book is available from the British Library.

ISBN 978 0 7524 3391 2

Typesetting and origination by
Tempus Publishing Limited.
Printed in Great Britain.

Contents

	Acknowledgements	6
	Introduction	7
one	BC: Before Coal	9
two	Early Mining	19
three	The Village Grows	39
four	Health and Welfare	59
five	People and Places	73
six	Up The Street	89
seven	Pit Work	101
eight	End of an Era	119

Acknowledgements

Thanks are due to the many photographers who spent years accumulating images of Ashington, many of which are included here. These include Johnnie Biggs and Jackie Laws, the two official photographers for the Ashington Coal Company and later the NCB; names from the past such as Pentland and Curry who took wonderful images of the town and its people, as did Alan G. Dickson, Reuben Daglish, Jack Wallace, Bob Hostler and other talented members of the Ashington Co-op Camera Club. Thanks are also due to the *Newcastle Journal and Evening Chronicle*, Northumberland Records Office, Wansbeck District Council and Woodhorn Colliery Museum. Thanks to calligrapher Edna Ralph who drew the 1849 map, and Jim Slaughter, illustrator of the Vin Kearney poem. Also to individuals who loaned photographs including: Neil Taylor, Ernie Slaughter, Joyce Robertson, Edna Ralph, Tommy Todd, Joy Warne, Winnie Barron, Jessie Langdown, George Nairn, John Tickner, Joan Hydes, Peggy Neary, Norman Barker, Mrs Ken Massen, Thornton Armstrong, Joyce Ferrie, Winnie Barron, Harry Badiali, Ronnie Harrison, John Crawford, Ronnie Patterson, Bill and Jean Harrison, Jean and Jack Leithead, Ann Mackintosh, Harry Speight, Neil Stevenson, Ray Scott, Mrs Carr, Ray Sewell, Joe Mawson, and Adrian Laws, with apologies to others who I may have inadvertently omitted.

EAST SCHOOLS. HIRST, ASHINGTON. 1794.

The East School changed its name to Alexandra First School in 1974 and closed completely in 2004.

Introduction

In the early 1800s Ashington was in the Parish of Bothal which was responsible for every parcel of land from Morpeth to Seaton Hirst, including the farmsteads at Ashington. At the heart of Bothal Village stood its magnificent fourteenth century castle, latterly owned in succession by the Dukes of Portland.

In the late 1700s, coal mining here only existed in small drift mines cut into the banks of the River Wansbeck. With permission from the 5th Duke of Portland there had been exploratory borings for coal in the Black Close area (near Stakeford Bank) but they were abandoned when a fault was discovered in the strata named the 'Stakeford Dyke' which rendered the proceedings there less than viable.

The dramatic change from farmland to a blighted industrial landscape began in 1847 when a shaft was sunk in what is now known as Ellington Road Ends on land owned by the Duke of Portland. That mine was christened 'Fell 'em Doon'. With the further development of pits at Woodhorn, Linton, Ellington and Lynemouth, this ultimately transformed East Northumberland and established Ashington's position as the pre-eminent town in the industry, justifying the audacious title of 'The Biggest Mining Village in the World'.

Miners came to Ashington from throughout the UK as tin mines closed in Cornwall and lead mines in Cumberland were worked out. From Ireland, many escaped the potato famine to settle here, expanding the town's population from about fifty in 1826 to over 7,000 by the beginning of the twentieth century. In 1851 there were no houses at all in Ashington. Soon there were 665 dwellings built to accommodate Ashington miners.

Development in the Hirst area followed with the sinking of Woodhorn and Linton collieries in the 1890s. By the early 1900s, the Hirst population had grown to 15,600 outstripping that of Ashington by over 8,000. The rapid inward migration of families created an enormous demand for housing. This was met by the same companies who owned the mines. The Ashington Coal Company (ACC) was formed soon after the Ashington group of collieries was established in the 1860s. The company's two leaders were Darlington-born Quaker Jonathan Priestman, mine owner and banker, and William Milburn, a Yorkshire entrepreneur with interests in real estate and shipping.

The Duke of Portland (family name Bentinck) took on the role of benefactor by bestowing huge tracts of land to the local council for building purposes when that body was formed in 1896. The Bentinck and Priestman families helped shape the pit communities of Ashington and Hirst. The 3rd Duke of Portland held the top position in the land when he became Prime Minister during the reign of George III. The wealthy Duke and his descendants held lands the length and breadth of Britain. Their ancestral seat was at Welbeck Castle in Nottinghamshire. Another of William Bentinck's titles was Earl of Titchfield. He owned an estate in Scotland called Langwell Lodge.

Ashington residents will recognise these names incorporated into the present-day streets of Duke Street, Portland Terrace, Langwell Crescent, Titchfield Terrace and

Welbeck Road. One of the 7th Duke's sons, John, had the middle name of Morven, hence Morven Place. Naturally the town's first hostelry was named The Portland Arms and the Colliers' football team are at present (2004) playing on Portland Park where they have been since around 1912, having bought the land outright from the Duke in December 1920 for £1,300.

The Bothal estate was centred on the Portland's family seat at Bothal Castle (usually occupied by their estate agent, a member of the Sample family). But it was the coal *under* this estate that led to the creation of modern Ashington. The town began to take shape when, as well as the sales of building plots and urban properties, several thousand acres of outlying portions were sold in the years immediately after the First World War at a time when large landowners were, in general, selling off peripheral lands and estates, usually to sitting tenants.

As well as the influence of the Duke of Portland on local affairs, the Priestmans (a family of Quakers from Darlington) were also instrumental in shaping the way of life of every man, woman and child in Ashington. The residents (who were also their workforce and tenants) were told by the ACC where and how they should live. Miners were constantly harangued because of what was perceived as their excessive drinking habits. The result was that no alcohol was allowed to be sold in Ashington for many years after the collieries got under way.

Land in the Hirst part of town, east of the railway station, was purchased by Milburn Estates. It was this family that gave us the name Milburn Road, and for many years a family member had to 'ride the bounds' of his estate, cordoning off the road at the North Seaton Hotel and also at the Hirst North School corner, so preserving his rights of ownership. The terraced houses of Hirst were laid out in a grid pattern, which was designed to facilitate rapid construction. This simple layout (similar to that used down the pit) was designed around a network of 2ft gauge railway tracks, laid out for leading bricks and other building materials to the construction sites.

The houses at Hirst were constructed with their backyards and outside toilets facing the tracks which traversed every back lane. When the houses were finally occupied, the railway was then used for leading the miners' concessionary coal during the day and taking away refuse from the middens and earth closets at night. The excrement extracted was led to a farm down Lintonville, just north of Portland Park, and spread across a field that was said to yield the most enormous potatoes ever seen.

Since the halcyon days of the 1950s when miners were top of the industrial wages league, the coalmines of Ashington and district have closed one by one (only Ellington Pit remains in 2004) each closure accompanied by fearful prognostications that the town would never be the same again. More recently, the disastrous coal strike of 1984/85 led to huge rifts in communities and families. But mining people around here are a resilient bunch, used to the hard knocks that have come their way for the last two centuries. The lure of black diamonds was the catalyst that brought these hard-working people to live in this region, even though many of them were destined to suffer premature and violent death. This book celebrates coal and, in particular, the coalminers of Ashington.

Mike Kirkup
August 2004

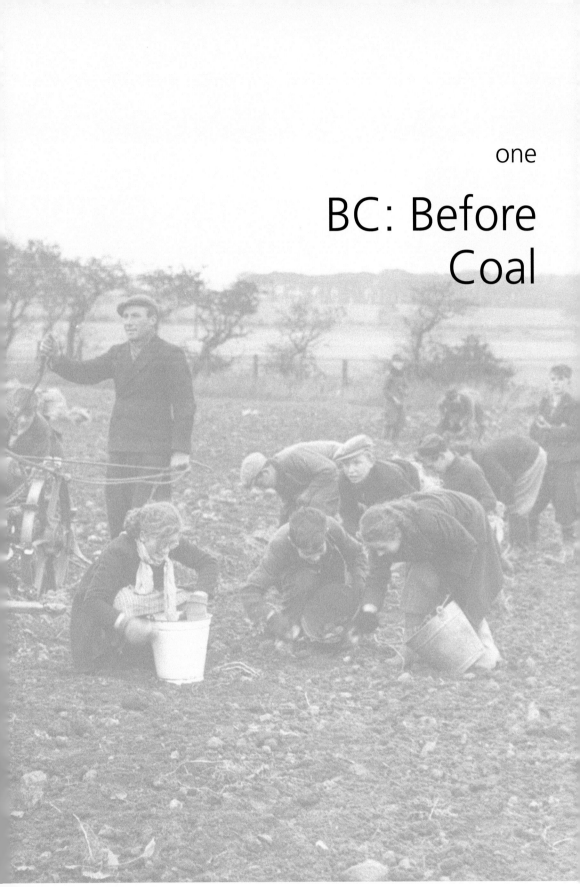

one

BC: Before Coal

Mouth of the River Wansbeck. The name 'Ashington', as it is spelled today, did not exist until about 300 years ago, but there was reference to an 'Essende' as early as 1170. It is possible that name was derived from Aesce, a Saxon marauder, who sailed his ship across the North Sea in the sixth century, found himself at the mouth of the River Wansbeck (now called Sandy Bay), navigated as far upriver as he could to Sheepwash, then settled in a fertile valley near the river bank.

Oldest stonework in Ashington. Much of what we now know as Ashington was fashioned from the mid-nineteenth century onwards. Up to the 1840s there had only been farmland and a few farm buildings. The section of wall above showing gaps that could have been a window and a fireplace, is reckoned to be over 200 years old. It stands in a field opposite Ashington Farm, situated on the road to Sheepwash.

Ashington Farm. The building has changed very little since it was erected. In the eighteenth century, the Revd John Wallis in his History of Northumberland wrote 'Ashington, which was one of the manors of barony of Bothall, and now belongs to George Sandiford Crow Esq, stands on an eminence, well sheltered with tall forest trees ... the grounds sloping regularly to a bank of oaks by the River Wansbeck.'

BOTHAL CASTLE, NORTHUMBERLAND.   Copyright.   THE DUKE OF PORTLAND.

Bothal Castle and 5th Duke of Portland, *c.* 1930. The original structure was built around 1150 for the Ogle family. In 1343 permission was granted to Sir Robert de Ogle to 'crenellate' (erect battlements) and the gate tower with its armorial shields was also built that year. In the eighteenth century, and by now owned by the Portlands (family name Bentinck), it was recorded that the castle was in a 'ruinous state' and restoration was carried out by the Duke of Portland's agents, called Sample.

Lady Chapel Well, Bothal Woods, Morpeth.

A holy well in Bothal Woods. The woods around Bothal Village contained a number of such wells and the river walks provided a welcome breath of fresh air for the mining communities of nearby Ashington and Pegswood. In 1821 Bothal Parish contained within its boundaries, Ashington, Pegswood, Longhirst, Old Moor and Shipwash. The main industry then was Ashington Quarry.

Sleepy amlet of Sheepwash, or Shipwash as it was once called because this was the furthest point to which ships could be safely navigated up the River Wansbeck from the inlet. It was here that the ships arriving to pick up stones from the quarry were 'washed down'. Hence Ship-wash.

Sheepwash Woods. This was a magic place for Ashington youngsters who were cooped up in dreary classrooms for the week. Here the adventurous youth could pretend to be Tarzan, tying a rope to one of the stout branches of a tree and swinging out dangerously low over the River Wansbeck.

Bothal Barns Farm. Located on the road from Cooper's shop to Bothal Village, this is still a working farm and probably shows little change from when it was worked and occupied over a hundred years ago. But even this farmland was blighted when Ashington Coal Company sank a drift mine here in the early twentieth century.

Coney Garth Farm. The pleasant acreage around this farm with its grazing sheep can still be seen by travellers on the Pegswood Road. Like its near neighbour at Bothal, Coney Garth Drift provided yet another access into the mine, this time to the Duke Pit of Ashington Colliery. These drift mines, plunged deep into the Ashington countryside, provided easy access for miners.

Above: Bothal Village. Nestling about a mile from Ashington, deep in a sleepy hollow, Bothal Village with its half dozen stone cottages is almost like the land that time forgot. Here, a gentleman watches his lady friend picking wild flowers.

Right: The Sample family plot. Standing within Bothal churchyard, this monument commemorates the lives of those who acted as land agents for successive Dukes of Portland in what was a high-profile, hectic period shortly before and after coal was discovered on the Duke's land. The vicar of Bothal at the time, the Reverend William Ellis, was a nephew of one of the Bentinck family who owned the castle.

Bothal stepping stones. This was always a favourite haunt of young children after the Second World War; even a young Sir Bobby Charlton – then living in Beatrice Street, Ashington – admitted to catching minnows here in a jam jar in the late 1940s.

Bridge crossing at Bothal. It was never more than a rickety, precarious way of getting across the river, but it was (and still is) an access to School Cottage. The original Bothal School dates back to 1725 when the Earl of Oxford, then owner of the estate that included Bothal Village, decreed that a school should be erected. He set aside £80, the interest from which was to be the salary of a schoolmaster for teaching eight pupils yearly.

OLD CASTLE HIRST

Hirst Castle, *c.* 1890. Farm buildings were the only structures to be seen in Ashington at the beginning of the nineteenth century and this was also the case at Hirst, a name derived from the Old English word 'Hyrste' meaning a wood. Part of Hirst was in Bothal Parish and part in Woodhorn Parish. One significant dwelling here was Hirst Castle, so called because of battlements that were built on to the farmhouse, said to be protection against cattle marauders. The first recorded mention of Hirst is in *Memoirs of the Missionary Priests of the Roman Church* where it was observed that 'George Errington, gent, born at Hirst, was put to death in York on 29 September 1536 for trying to convert a Protestant'. There was a rumour that Hirst Castle was linked to Bothal Castle by an underground tunnel, but this was never proven. What was known was that a miser called Jobson lived next door who was 'given to wearing a long black and white plaid which streamed out in the wind when he walked'. According to the late Miss Vida Sample, a local teacher, two houses were built right opposite Hirst Castle for a couple of local medical men, Dr Trotter and Dr Goldie. One house was converted into the Hirst Universal Club, now re-named Hyrste Castle. The original Hirst Castle was demolished early in the twentieth century, but its name was preserved when nearby Castle Terrace was built and named accordingly.

Woodhorn Grange Farm, 1954. Helped by his two trusty shirehorses, Bull and Ben, Thornton Armstrong, a Newbiggin-born man, is unearthing the spuds so that local schoolchildren (off school during Blackberry Week) can gather them in pails to be emptied into sacks. For this back-breaking chore they were paid a few pennies plus the occasional pail of 'tetties' to take home to boost the family pantry.

Woodhorn Mill, *c.* 1950. Built in 1846 by Robert Hindhaugh, this mill was said to be a landmark for vessels approaching Newbiggin Bay. It was recorded in *North Country Lore and Legend* by J.R. Boyle that 'Woodhorn is one of the bleak seaboard parishes in Northumberland. The name means the "wooded horn" or ness of land jutting out into the sea.' When it was a working mill in the nineteenth century, one of the mill-keeper's daughters was swept out of the top aperture when her long dress was caught up in the sails. She was killed outright when flung down on to the ground.

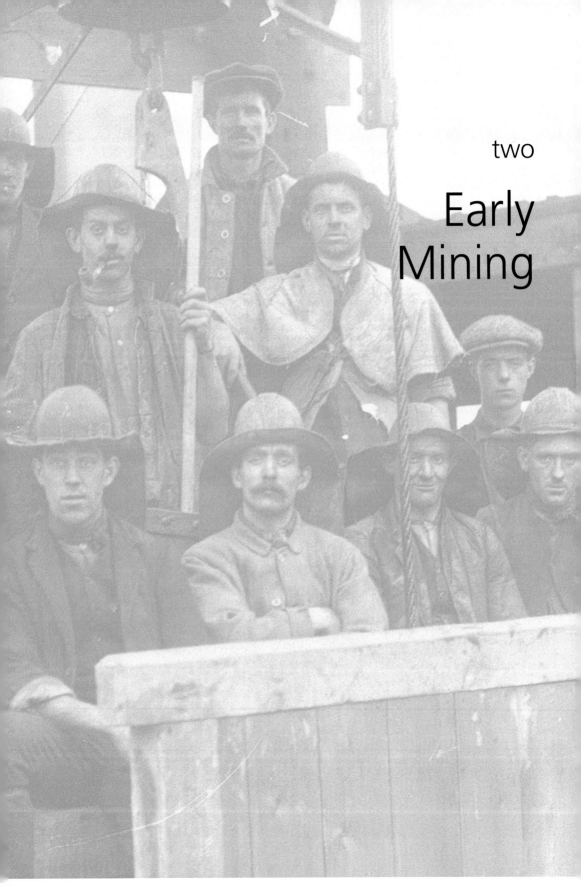

two

Early Mining

New Moor

North Hurst

RKWORTH BRANCH

NEWBIGGIN BRANCH

PORTLAND
RTH HARTLEY
COLL?

Hurst

Moor House

Spital Ho.

down

High Black Close

B. & T. R.

North Seaton

ington

INTENDED
WINNING

Lane End

NORTH SEATON
COLL?

Sheepwash

Low
Black Close

NORTH SEATON
STATION

High Quay

Low Quay

swell
Hill

Stake Ford
Ho.

Marshes
Houses

Cambois

WEST SLEEKBURN
COLLIERY

ey Hill

BARRINGTON
NEW WINNING

CAMBOIS NEW
WINNING

West Sleekburn

Sleekburn

RANCH

East Sleekburn

BEDLINGTON
COLL?

BEDLINGTON
STATION

Above: Illustration of a Bell Pit. Towards the north–west boundary of the Ashington royalty, the upper coal seams outcropped into open fields and were worked sporadically as bell-pits by miners from very early times. Coal had been used as a form of fuel for hundreds of years. Initially, a man would find a suitable field and begin digging with a spade until he reached a coal seam. Some Northumberland seams were extremely shallow and might occur only a few feet from the surface. With just a candle to light his way, the first primitive miner used a sharp instrument of some kind (perhaps an axe) to loosen and break up the coal into manageable lumps which he then loaded into a bag or basket and carried to the surface. This drawing shows a bell pit (the name comes from its shape) where the miner has erected a platform to reach the coal. No roof supports were needed and, after the coal was worked out, the miner simply found another spot on the field and began digging again.

Previous page: From an 1849 Map. Drawn shortly after the Portland North Hartley Colliery opened at Fell'em Doon (note the posher spelling of Fell'em Down). Ashington is shown as an 'Intended Winning', meaning where pit shafts were about to be sunk in search of coal. A railway line went only as far as North Seaton where a mineral line extended to that colliery, and it was not until about twenty years later that a line was connected to Hirst (later changed to Ashington) Station. Although there were many collieries in the vicinity: Longhirst, West Sleekburn, Choppington etc., it was predominantly rural at Ashington and its nearby farms of 'Cunning Garth' (Coney Garth), Sparrow House and High Black Close. An agreement to build a branch line towards Ashington Colliery was made on 31 May 1854 between the Duke of Portland and the Blyth and Tyne Railway. Under the agreement, the Duke would extend this line to the colliery and maintain it. This enabled coal to be transported quickly to the coast for shipment.

Shaft sinkers, 1909. Seated far left smoking a pipe was Ellington man, Ned Grieves. These were a brave bunch of men who travelled all over the North East selling their expertise to the wealthy coalowners. Houses were built next to the mine to accommodate the sinkers and their families, often called Sinkers Row. It was a hazardous occupation and many men perished through falling headlong into the shaft.

Ashington Colliery, 1920. According to a 1924 brochure prepared by Ashington Coal Company, its directors were Lewis Priestman, Fred Milburn, Charles Pumphrey, G.L. Wanless, A.W. Milburn and Sir Leonard Milburn Bart, with Ridley Warham as managing director. Their head office was at Milburn House, Dean Street, Newcastle.

Above: Bothal shaft bottom, *c.* 1920. Ashington Colliery, whose first shaft 'The Bothal' was sunk in 1866, then mined from five coal seams, the High Main being the shallowest at 24 fathoms (144ft), the Main Seam, Yard Seam, Five Quarter, and Low Main, the deepest seam at 88 fathoms (528ft). The Yard Seam was an exceptionally good house coal, and sold under the name of 'Ashington Wallsend'.

Left: Hand drilling, *c.* 1920. Much of the early means of production at Ashington Colliery was labour intensive. One arduous task was that of drilling a hole about 4ft in depth into which explosives could be placed in order to blast the coal down from the hard seam. This man is working by the light from a candle suspended from the pit prop behind him.

Right: Hewing, *c.* 1920. One of the highest paid workers underground in the early days was the hewer, instantly recognisable by his cut-off trousers. Using a steel pick, the hewer had to hack away at any part of the coal seam that had not been brought down by the explosives. This man is working by the light of one of the first safety lamps in a relatively high seam, possible the Five Quarter.

Below: Tub filling, *c.* 1920. Early coal workings used a bord (roof support) and pillar method which entailed extracting a wedge of coal but leaving sufficient coal to hold up the roof. This filler is attempting to place a larger than usual lump of coal on to his shovel. In reality this would never happen – he would simply pick up a piece as large as this and 'hoy' it into the tub which held about half a ton of coal.

Tipplers emptying tubs from the Duke Pit, *c.* 1920. Once the coal tubs had been brought up the shaft, they were directed to a set of 'tipplers' which upended the contents on to a screening belt. A coal company diary reveals that in November 1886, the recreation ground was fenced in and a Hall was built there three years later for which the Duke of Portland gave £100, and the ACC donated £100 plus free bricks from their own kiln.

Screening the coal, *c.* 1920. Of all the jobs at the pit, working on the screens was the most soul destroying. Imagine standing for seven and a half hours picking bits of stone from a moving metal belt that threw up clouds of dust into your eyes as your ears were blasted by the continuous din. New recruits to the pit got their first introduction to pit work on the hellish screens.

Arc wall coal cutting, *c.* 1920. For many years the ACC had devoted a great deal of attention to the development of machine mining, so much so that by the 1920s, seventy per cent of the output was obtained by mechanical methods. This is how the coal winning process was explained in a 1924 brochure: 'The general method of machine working involves undercutting the coal by means of a cutting machine, then drilling holes in the coal.'

Filling on to a conveyor belt, *c.* 1920. When conveyor filling was introduced, coal production increased considerably. Coal shipped from Ashington Colliery to Blyth Staiths in 1886 was 144,983 tons; but seven years later this had risen to 729,247 tons. The village population was also rising. According to the census of 1801, there were only 56 people then living in the Ashington area which also included Sheepwash. The population probably peaked in 1931 when 29,847 folk were resident in Ashington.

Fitters bay, *c.* 1920. The term 'colliery mechanic' is a generic term and by the 1870s it referred to a number of trades employed at a colliery, namely blacksmiths, boilermakers, bricklayers, engine wrights, fitters, joiners, masons, painters, plumbers, saddlers, sawyers, tub-menders and wagon wrights, and to their mates, helpers or assistants, and to the apprentices and boys who served with those trades. When electricity began to be introduced into the mines around 1910, the colliery electrician became almost indispensable to the smooth running of the mines, especially during the two world wars and in the high-tech world of the 1970s to '90s. A number of local men held positions of importance in the Northumberland Colliery Mechanics Association, including John M. Gillians, Tom Fox, George Brownrigg and Bob Wallace who all worked at Ashington Colliery, Arnold Emery of Lynemouth and George Whitfield of Ellington Pit.

Blacksmiths' bay at main workshops, *c.* 1920. This included blacksmiths and strikers. One of their jobs was that of farrier down the pit, kept busy with the shoeing of pit ponies. In 1924 there were 1,065 ponies working underground at the four pits of Ashington, Woodhorn, Linton and Ellington, ranging in size from 9 to 14 hands and consuming 2,600 tons of 'choppy' (chopped-up wheat and oats) per annum.

Electricians workshop, *c.* 1920. By 1924, the total length of electric power cables in use above and below ground at the ACC pits was a staggering 130 miles and the number of Board of Trade units of electrical power used each year amounted to 24 million. In modern times, the colliery electrician had to cope with the transmission and distribution of energy, and the utilisation of all types of equipment, such as cable-jointing, switchgear motors and control gear, signalling systems and telephone communications.

Woodhorn Colliery, 1924. Old-timer Sam Snow saw its beginning. He said: 'In the month of May 1894, I saw Mr Richardson (colliery engineer after whom Richardson Street is named) cut the sod for No. 1 Pit. As I passed over the railway line by the path to Woodhorn Village, I had seen a group of men laying down the rail points and making ready for the sidings for Woodhorn Colliery on 1 April.'

Woodhorn Colliery, 1960. Ask anyone who worked at Woodhorn, and they will tell you that it was a friendly family pit. Fathers, sons and brothers worked side by side, such as the Sparrow brothers, Mick who was a cutter-man, and Harry and Fred who were 'drifters'.

Linton Colliery, 1930. Before Linton Colliery was sunk in 1896, there were only twelve dwellings and a population of fifty-nine in the village. Occupations then were mainly farming related. When the first shaft was sunk, three rows of houses were built, and a corrugated iron and timber hut was erected next to the manager's house – this doubled as a church on Sundays and a school through the week.

Linton Colliery No. 2, Winder House and Headgear Foundations, 1952. Annie Horn was organiser of the Linton Pathfinders Youth Group in the 1950s when she wrote this piece for a speaking contest in Leicester: 'If you look at the map of Northumberland, I doubt if you will see Linton, which is the place where I live. I doubt also that you would bother to look for it … and yet to me and my family, and most of the villagers, Linton is a remarkable little village.'

Ellington Colliery, *c.* 1911. This was the third colliery to be sunk by ACC in 1909. Three colliery rows were built to house the workforce, most of whom had to travel from Ashington via the tankey. First Row was mainly for the mine officials and was the last to be built.

Ellington Baths, 1924. These were the first pithead baths to be opened in Northumberland. As no lockers were provided, the men and boys had to string their clothes together and use a pulley system to hoist them to the ceiling where long pipes filled with hot water dried them off ready for the next shift. Many miners were self conscious and preferred not to use the baths at all and so risk being the butt of many jibes.

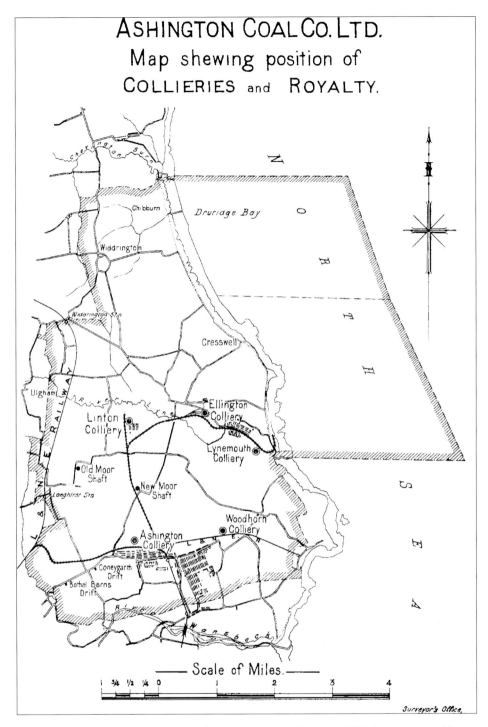

Map of Ashington Coal Company's collieries, 1924. On 13 August 1888, it was arranged by the Ashington Coal Company with co-operation from the Reverend W. Ellis for leave to bring coals through underneath the Holy Sepulchre churchyard's north-west corner with the Low Main Seam under the Black Plantation for a fee of £40 per annum.

Lynemouth Colliery, 1952. Plans to open Lynemouth Pit were made in the early 1920s, but lack of trade plus a devastating six-month stoppage in 1926 meant that coal was not drawn from this 'model pit' until 1934. By then all the infrastructure was in place; houses for miners and their families were the best in the district with indoor plumbing, long gardens and an open aspect.

Ashington Colliery, 1924. From this aerial view it is noticeable how close the colliery streets of Fifth and Sixth Row, seen on the right, were to the pit yard itself. In the foreground is the recreation ground and you can spot the Rec Bridge that allowed access for footballers and rugby players on a Saturday afternoon; note also the football pitches and tennis courts.

Tankey No. 38, *c*. 1950. Thirty years later, this might well have been the same train seen in the top picture on p. 34, now pulling wagons marked NCB (National Coal Board). Certainly it is on the same approach to the rail crossing at Piggy Moor Lonnen (Lintonville). These huge engines were much loved by their drivers who built up an affinity with the same engine during each shift.

Linton Colliery from the air, 1924. Originally there was only one coal winding shaft, drawing coal from the Yard Seam level at depth of 49 fathoms (294ft) producing 1,900 tons a day. An outlying shaft was sunk at Old Moor for the purpose of putting men down close to their work. Redevelopment occurred in 1952 when a further shaft was sunk in the pit yard.

Ellington Colliery aerial view, 1924. The three rows of colliery houses are seen at the top of the photograph, looking north. A school here for local children was described as 'a dreadful mish-mash of wooden huts'. Pupils and teachers alike could hardly wait to see the back of it when a new school was built at Linton in 1926.

Lynemouth Colliery, 1953. This aerial shot shows how much modernisation had taken place in the early 1950s on this vast complex. Lynemouth was to be the 'jewel in the crown' of all the region's collieries. Miners at Ashington cast envious eyes towards the coastal pit with thick seams of coal running way out under the North Sea. Underground, it had the most modern equipment ever seen in a coalmine.

Newbiggin Colliery under construction in 1908. Although not strictly attached to the Ashington Coal Company, it is common knowledge that many Ashington men moved into the seaside village when that colliery opened. It was also easier to get a much more superior colliery house there. In spite of this, Newbiggin remained an old-fashioned mine and it was no surprise when it closed in November 1967.

North Seaton Colliery, September 1939. Another pit that was not part of the ACC group, but was owned by the Cowpen Coal Company. This photograph shows the scene after an extensive outbreak of fire and subsequent explosion in the Low Main Seam near the shaft bottom. The three vehicles standing in the pit yard were from the Mines Rescue Brigade. Luckily no one was injured in the incident.

Pegswood Colliery and village, 1950. Pegswood was another pit village that lived under the shadow of its pit heaps. The colliery opened in 1868 and the last group of men came to bank in February 1969. One of the colliery rows was named 'Bentinck', after the family name of the Duke of Portland who owned the royalty for the pit.

Bomarsund Colliery, c. 1920. Pronounced 'Boomer', this colliery opened in 1905. It gained the unusual name, it is said, because a battle was raging at the town of Bomarsund in the Baltic at the time involving British soldiers. The Boomer closed in October 1965 after drawing coal for exactly sixty years.

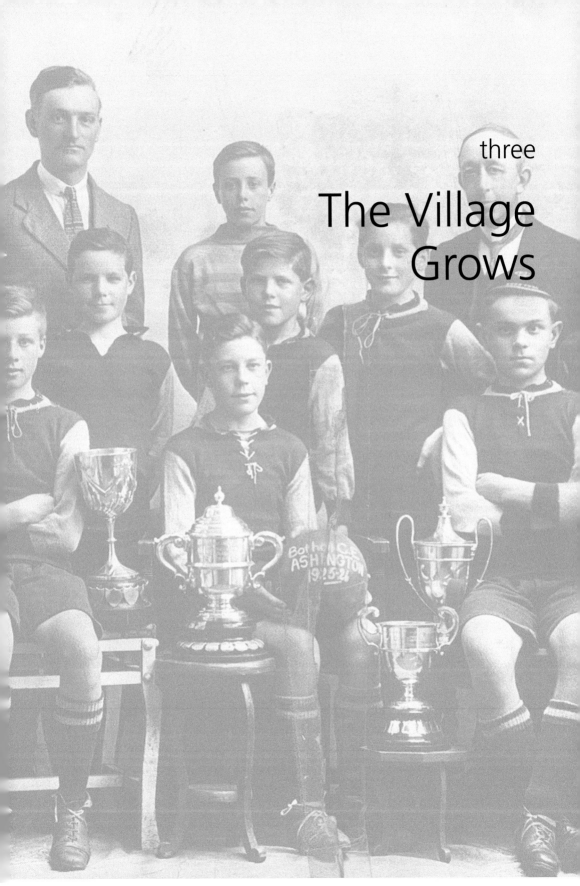

three

The Village Grows

Long Row, *c.* 1900. In 1851 there were no colliery houses at all in Ashington. Building of the Long Row began in 1853 and four years later thirty-three plain back-to-back houses had been built. They consisted of two storeys of four rooms each, but a dividing wall separated the front two rooms from the back two rooms. This meant that two families occupied each of the thirty-three houses.

Cross Row, *c.* 1960. The erection of Cross Row's fifteen houses was completed in 1861 at the same time as the additions to the Long Row. At that time seventy-four families were housed at Ashington Colliery, as the new village was called. The dwellings boasted long gardens where miners could grow their own produce.

Tenth Row. By 1890, all of Ashington Colliery's 665 houses at the 'top end' had been built in eleven rows. It was in that year that the first eight houses were built in the Hirst. Ten years later, at the turn of the century, houses from Woodhorn Road to Second Avenue and to Chestnut Street from Laburnum Terrace had been built. Part of North Seaton Road (then called Hexham Terrace) had also been erected by then. In 1891, a census was carried out at Ashington Colliery giving the breakdown of house occupancy. This showed that 846 houses had been built. That figure included all the rows from First to Eleventh, Long Row, Cross Row and Stable Row, also a group of dwellings called the Six Houses, built for the original shaft sinkers. At that time only 775 houses were occupied. Accommodation varied immensely – of the 100 houses built in the Tenth Row, sixty-three were two-roomed dwellings, while the remainder had a third room added. These eleven colliery rows west of the railway line were huddled around the pit yard itself. The long depressing streets of late nineteenth-century terraced houses afforded rent-free accommodation to families that had a pieceworker working underground at the pit. The waiting list for the colliery houses owned by Ashington Coal Company could be as much as seven years.

Sheepwash Bridge collapses, 1894. The bridge at Sheepwash provided the only means of road access into Ashington for horse-drawn carts laden with provisions from Choppington and Cramlington. Reporting on the storm of '94, a local newspaper wrote, 'It was as a result of floods following frosts that the old bridge at Sheepwash was broken by the turbulent waters of the swollen Wansbeck.'

Sheepwash Bridge, c. 1900. In 1886 a pump house (to the right) was erected at Sheepwash to enable water to be pumped from the River Wansbeck to Ashington Colliery. For many years the people of Ashington had to drink water that was pumped out of the mine. In his 1919 medical report, Dr Frank Gairdner the colliery physician wrote: 'The Ashington Pit supply of water, being of such questionable quality, chlorination of it was commenced in October 1919.'

Stakeford Bridge, *c.* 1910. When part of Sheepwash Bridge was swept away by a great storm it became imperative to build another bridge so that traders could continue coming into Ashington. Miners and businessmen from Ashington and Bedlington agreed that the most convenient site for a new bridge was at Stakeford where the river until then had only been accessible by a hand-hauled ferry.

Wheatley's ferry, *c.* 1914. Prior to the new bridge being opened, the only way to cross the River Wansbeck at this particular point was to either wait for low tide and wade across, or to use a ferry service which operated from the Cambois side of the river. This was worked by hauling a small boat attached to a chain and was managed by Mr Wheatley, becoming known as Wheatley's Ferry.

Above: Portland Arms Hotel, *c.* 1900. On 1 May 1890 land extending to 5,237 square yards was bought for £724 16s 3d (payable in instalments) with the intention of building 'Ashington Hotel' (later re-named The Portland Arms). The building of Ashington's first hotel was carried out by Matthew Hogarth of Choppington, to a design by William Glover. The purchaser was named as Thomas Forbes of the Highland Hotel, North Shields. Rent was set initially at £800, rising in 1895 to £1,500 per annum. But Hogarth had underestimated the building costs and the final bill came to £6,235. When the lease came up for renewal in 1902, Thomas Forbes sent a letter to the Duke concerning reduced income at the Portland 'thanks to the growth of workingmen's clubs, resulting in heightened competition.'

Left: Portland Arms beer bottle, *c.* 1900. Thomas Forbes arranged with a brewery for beer to be delivered in barrels by train to Ashington Station. He then bottled it with his own logo. On 9 December 1892, the Ashington Coal Company resolved to make use of the Portland Arms Hotel for Ashington miners' meetings.

Typical Colliery House Kitchen, *c.* 1930. This was an exhibit at Woodhorn Colliery Museum and showed where a miner's wife did most of her household chores. On the table is a griddle and some pastry for making griddle (or girdle) scones. This would be picked up and placed directly onto the fire.

Seaton Hirst Church, *c.* 1905. The church of St John at Seaton Hirst was consecrated on 11 November 1897. By 1905 the Parish of Seaton Hirst had been formed and finally divided from the old Woodhorn Parish. In 1891 the population of the area was only fifty-seven, but by 1903 this figure had risen dramatically to over 9,000, an increase brought about by the massive building programme of colliery houses at Hirst.

Priestman's Institute, *c.* 1920. This was one of the amenities built in the 1890s for the miners of Hirst. The Tute had six immaculately-kept billiard tables as well as facilities for darts, dominoes and cards. A well-stocked library and delivery of daily newspapers meant that the members were kept well informed of local and national news.

Hirst Park, Ashington.

Hirst Flower Park, *c.* 1930. Colliery houses were packed together in long rows at Hirst so it was recognised that an area needed to be set aside where the mining community could enjoy some space to contemplate a better life and at the same time enjoy the colour afforded by a flower park. The park opened in 1914 and contained not only hundreds of different plants, but sporting facilities for lovers of bowls and tennis.

Market Place (High Market), *c.* 1900. Shops first began to appear in Ashington around 1890 in the High Market area, or Market Place as it was known. One of the first shops belonged to John Wilkinson, initially a newsagent and later an auctioneer and printer. The first shop on the right was owned by William Wilson who, like Wilkinson, became one of Ashington's first councillors in 1896.

Longhirst Station

Longhirst Station, *c.* 1900. John Wilkinson, who later became an alderman, had to send a horse and cart each morning to this station to pick up his daily national newspapers. On John's first day of opening shop, the day's takings amounted to only three shillings and sevenpence ha'penny.

Ashington Railway Station, *c.* 1890. The Ashington Coal Company complex soon linked up with the Blyth and Tyne railway network which provided a means of getting coal quickly from the mine to the coal staithes at Blyth and on Tyneside. A railway station was opened at Ashington in 1878 called 'Hirst' but in 1889, at the insistence of the ACC, it was renamed.

L.N.E.R.
NEW REDUCED FARES
BY ANY TRAIN
BETWEEN
ASHINGTON

AND		THIRD Single	THIRD Ret.			THIRD Single	THIRD Ret.
Backworth	.	1/–	1/6	Newbiggin . .		2d.	3d.
Bebside .	.	4d.	6d.	Newcastle (Central) .		1/3	1/9
Bedlington	.	3d.	5d.	Manors . .	.	1/3	1/9
Benton .	.	1/–	1/6	Newsham . .	.	8d.	1/–
Blyth .	.	7d.	10d.	North Seaton .	.	1d.	2d.
Choppington	.	5d.	7d.				
Hartley .	.	10d.	1/4	Seaton Delavel	.	11d.	1/5
Hepscott.	.	6d.	10d.	Seghill . .	.	1/–	1/6
Jesmond.	.	1/3	1/9	South Gosforth	.	1/3	1/9
Morpeth .	.	8d.	1/–	West Jesmond	.	1/3	1/9

37 Trains each Weekday—Ashington Newbiggin North Seaton and Newcastle

For full details see bills at Stations and on "Cheap Rail Travel" Boards

Train timetable, 1928. An *Ashington Collieries Magazine* advertisement from December 1928. A whopping thirty-seven trains a day ran between Ashington and outlying villages. Already the competition from United's buses was forcing LNER to rethink their prices, but the fare to Newbiggin of 3d return looks attractive, even in those days.

Holy Sepulchre, *c.* 1930. This church was built in 1887, and named after a church that once existed in Sheepwash. The Holy Sepulchre was built on two acres of land donated by the Duke of Portland who also gave £500 towards building costs. In May 1889, the induction of Reverend J. Lightfoot, formerly Curate of Bothal, was undertaken by the Bishop of Newcastle as the first vicar of Ashington.

Bothal School Football Team, 1926. The first school to be built in Ashington, the Bothal opened in 1873. Left to right, back row: I. Middlemiss, Mr William Cole, Craig Brown, Mr J. Gray (headmaster), Mr W. Lynn. Middle row: A. Cairns, ? Soulsby, J. Wedderburn, E. Vout, L. Hogg. Seated in front row: George Walker, George McDonald, Harry Bridge, Jim Pattison and Richard 'Dick' Lewis.

Jack Rodway's Rolley by Vin Kearney.

Noo Aa'll tell ye 'boot a rolley that was once of local fame
it belaanged tiv an Ashin'ton businessman, Jack Rodway was his name.

He charged a tanner for an hoor or half a croon a day
but ye shud hev seen the queer things that his rolley tyun away.

Noo Aa seen it loaded up one day wiv mats 'nd beds, the lot
and for its croonin' glory was a greet big chamber pot.

As it torned around a corner ye shud've hord the screams
when they lost their indoor toilet as it smashed tiv smithereens.

Noo it costs a bloomin' fortune ti send objects tiv the moon
but that rolley shifted *aall* the Horst for less than half a croon.

And when it cums ti my last day and St Peter caalls me name
Aa'll hitch a ride on Rodway's Rolley intiv the Haall of Fame.

(Illustration by Jim Slaughter. Last two lines added as a tribute to the great man himself: Vin Kearney).

The 'Top' Store, *c.* 1890. The Co-operative Movement reached Ashington in 1887 when a large store was opened beside the Holy Sepulchre church. Shopping at the 'Store' became a way of life for the miner's wife – it was she who did the shopping, but at first, it was only the male of the family who was allowed to become a member and be eligible for dividend on purchases.

Grand Hotel, *c.* 1900. Built in the 1890s, the Grand was an imposing building which dominated the centre of Ashington's main shopping street, and for many years provided the only public timepiece. The upstairs windows were made of stained glass depicting the coat of arms of famous Northumberland families such as the Percys and Ogles.

Grand Hotel looking north, *c.* 1910. It was at this side that the Grand's stables accommodated the horses of weary travellers who had arrived to stay for the night. A social club – the Grand Street – opened on the opposite side of the road. Shops here included Roulstone the tobacconist and the premises of Russell Cook's cousin, Stanley Cook, who specialised in selling pet food.

Grand Corner looking east, *c.* 1950. The Wallaw Cinema is seen on the left with the three shops that were leased out by owner Walter Lawson. Then there is a gap before the old United bus terminus, built in 1936 (now a Wetherspoons pub) and then the Store Arcade. Further along Woodhorn Road is the Central Hall, a landmark that is sadly no longer with us.

Ashington Co-op staff, 1950. Lined up on the steps of the Arcade, and ready for a day's outing, most of these folks worked for the greengrocery department at the Top Store. Top row includes Clemmy Quinn, Kathy Jenkins, Mary Lumb and Eddie Hart. Second top row: Mrs Cobbledick, Mrs Dobson, Mr McAvoy, Peggy Lawson, Elsie Flawell, Joyce Ferguson, Bertie Hindhaugh, and Cecil Scott. Front row: Jack Dobson, Joan Cobbledick, Mr McAvoy, Vera Cullingworth, Jean Stoker, Hazel Parkinson, Ruth Laidler and Tony Burt. Jean Stoker and Cecil Scott were married shortly afterwards.

Seaton Hirst Co-operative, Milburn Road, *c.* 1905. This was actually a branch of the North Seaton & Newbiggin Co-op, opened in 1900. You can see that no houses have been built on the other side of Milburn Road where a little girl plays in the wild grass.

Store Arcade, *c.* 1926. After the First World War, as the Duke of Portland continued to sell off chunks of land, larger sites were also changing hands at knock-down prices by today's standards. On 2 September 1919 Ashington Industrial Co-operative Society bought six properties from 23 to 28 Wansbeck Terrace, which included a greengrocer's store and a tripe house for the paltry sum of £697 19s 1d.

Site of Dungait's Farm, *c.* 1926. United Automobile Services Ltd bought a parcel of land on 19 September 1921 for £410 5s. This was to become their garage and, later, Ashington's first bus terminus, built on the site of James Dungait's Farm in 1936. Until then buses picked up passengers at stops along Station Road.

Arrowsmith's Corner, *c.* 1910. George Arrowsmith opened up a large department store at No. 2 Portland Buildings in the early 1900s. If that location sounds puzzling to present-day shoppers, it later became No. 4 Woodhorn Road. On 5 May 1919, George was able to buy his leasehold outright from the Duke of Portland for £115. He also owned a menswear shop on the other side of the road at No. 26 Station Road for which he paid £57 10s. No. 3 Portland Buildings was an ironmonger's shop (seen on right of photograph), Robert Walker paid £138 in April 1921 for the leasehold. The area at this crossroads – now in 2004 the busiest in Ashington – was called at various times Cook's Corner, or Arrowsmith's Corner, but the most popular name was The Grand Corner, a regular meeting place for women out shopping or men gathering before opening time at one of the three public houses or, by the 1920s, at one of the twenty social clubs then open for business in town. This vast amount of drinking establishments was later to earn Ashington the dubious title of 'Satan's Citadel'.

Woodhorn Road looking west, *c.* 1930. This was always a fine open road, mostly used by residents at the Hirst end of town on their way 'up the street'. The semi-detached houses on the right were much sought-after as being a prestigious part of town in which to live. Shops began to open on the left-hand side, such as the sub-post office at No. 55.

Laburnum Terrace, 1930. This became another shopping area with specialist shops and businesses, such as a dentist and pharmacist. The first retail shop was occupied at No. 1 by Hope Herriott in the 1920s, selling pit stockings for one shilling a pair. That shop was later taken over by Jimmy Main, selling the latest in motorbikes in the 1950s.

Newbiggin Road shops, *c.* 1910. There were limited retail outlets at North Seaton Colliery Village so shops began to sprout at the end of Newbiggin Road, opposite the North Seaton Hotel. R. Maughan's sweet shop, seen here, occupied one of the rare stone-built buildings in the area. Traders on the other side of Newbiggin Road included Granny Weddle who had a sweet shop next to the Hippodrome Theatre, and John Spedding, newsagent and sub-postmaster.

Council Chambers and Rescue Brigade Headquarters, *c.* 1920. Ashington Council was formed in 1896 and moved into these new premises on Station Bridge around 1912. The Durham and Northumberland Rescue Brigade built their headquarters next door in 1914. One of the first rescue attempts for these brave men was in August 1916 when a gas explosion at Woodhorn Colliery claimed the lives of thirteen men and one pit pony.

Wesleyan Central Hall, 1930. The Wesleyan Methodist Central Hall on Woodhorn Road – known originally as the New Mission Hall – opened in 1924. This became the venue for some of the most talented musicians and singers in the world. In 1930, Normanton Barron was persuaded to bring his Newbiggin Orchestra and Choral Union to the Central Hall where they performed Sunday evening concerts from the 1940s onwards until the building was summarily demolished in 1989.

Normanton Barron and Moira Anderson, *c.* 1975. Immediately after the Second World War, Normanton Barron booked world-famous celebrities to appear at the Central Hall. In the mid-1970s he was awarded a Rose Bowl by Ashington Council for achievement in the field of music. Scottish songstress and television regular, Moira Anderson was one of the last personalities commissioned by Normanton before he died in 1977.

four

Health and Welfare

Vol. II—No. 9.   SEPTEMBER, 1922.   Price 2d.

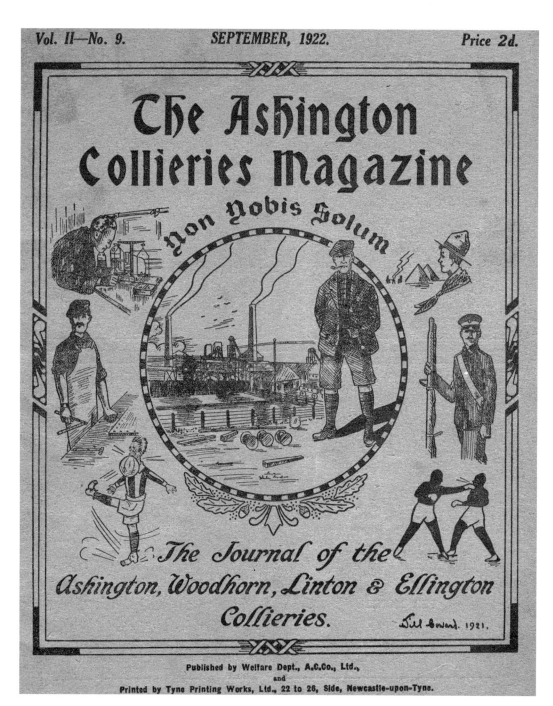

The Ashington Collieries Magazine

Non Nobis Solum

The Journal of the Ashington, Woodhorn, Linton & Ellington Collieries.

Bill Cowans. 1921.

Published by Welfare Dept., A.C.Co., Ltd.,
and
Printed by Tyne Printing Works, Ltd., 22 to 26, Side, Newcastle-upon-Tyne.

The Ashington Collieries Magazine, September 1922. The ACC published its own in-house magazines from 1920. Initially this was a high-brow publication containing articles on 'The Great Composers' and reports of parliamentary debates. But as the years progressed and new people like Alan Robson and Fred Reed were drafted into the Welfare Office, it featured more sport, jokes and cartoons. Drawings here by Will Robson with calligraphy by Bill Cowans. Note, Lynemouth Colliery was yet to open.

Right: Cartoon in *Collieries Magazine*, 1926. Drawn by James Leslie Brownrigg who later became a teacher at the Hirst South School. He drew a series of 'Pitmen's Jobs Illustrated'. The 'Back Overman' was the gaffer who kept the 'backshift'. Overmen could be recognised by their apparel; the black jacket and hat turned back to front, carrying a safety lamp and yardstick with which to measure a 'stretch' of coal.

Below: Billiard room at Hirst Welfare, *c.* 1922. The ACC began an extensive welfare scheme in 1920 that involved building recreation facilities near all of its five collieries. Football, cricket and hockey pitches were laid, as well as providing facilities for tennis, athletics, bicycle riding and bowls. The game of billiards was very popular with the miners who produced some skilful players from within their midst.

MINING TERMS ILLUSTRATED.

ON THE FLAT-SHEETS
THE "BACK OVERMAN"

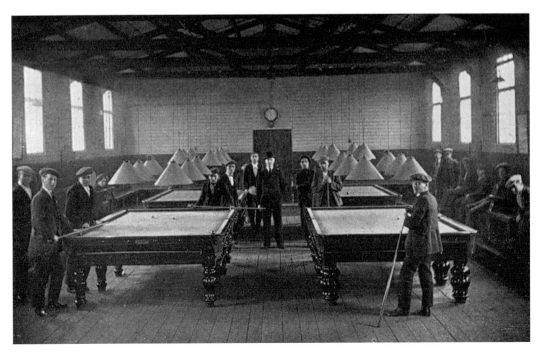

Children's playground at the 'Rec', c. 1922. An area was set aside for children at each of the area's welfare grounds. This was the first to be built on the recreation ground near Ashington Colliery. Pictured top left is a ride called the Ocean Wave, so named because, as it was propelled, it gave the impression of going up and down on a boat. The Banana Slide, bottom right, soared to an enormous height, but later had to be dismantled owing to the large number of accidents. As can be seen from the crowds, the rec was hugely popular with children who could hardly wait to get away from the clarty backstreets and out into the fresh air. Some other boisterous rides were the Pirate Ship and the Maypole as well as the usual swings and Tea Pot Lid. Present day legislation regarding health and safety render it doubtful that any of these rides would be acceptable today.

Gymnastics at Recreation Hall, *c.* 1922. Two men were employed to coach young lads in the art of boxing and gymnastics: George Clemenson and George Hindhaugh. George is seen here giving a helping hand to would-be gymnasts on the apparatus. On Saturday nights this hall doubled as a dance floor, often with music by Joe Dalkin and his Rhythm Boys.

St John's Ladies Priestman Division, *c.* 1930. The Lady Divisional Superintendent at the time was Mrs Thain who is possibly seated front centre. Other lady members from this era included Lady Ambulance Officer Miss Brown, Margaret Abbott, the sisters Ethel, Maud and Nina Pattison, Doris Robinson and Margaret Craigs. Coal Company official, Mr Fred Booth's wife was another member.

St John's Ambulance Brigade Headquarters (top) plus team, *c.* 1922. Because of the number of accidents both above and below the surface, the ACC built the Ambulance Brigade Headquarters near Ashington Hospital in the early 1920s and staffed it with volunteers – many of them miners – who had gained a first aid certificate.

Albion Road, Lynemouth, 1924. A statement in an official 1924 brochure said: 'Lynemouth is specially noteworthy as it is an entirely new village designed to house colliery workers so that they may enjoy all the amenities of living in a well laid out modern country village with ample gardens and well-made roads and footpaths.' The streets were named alphabetically, Albion being the first, then Boland Road and Chester Square etc.

Float at Salvation Army Headquarters on Station Road, 1927. On Boxing Day 1927, the Salvationists gave a dinner to 1,500 poor children in the Princess Ballroom. The farm at Ashington Colliery donated half a ton of potatoes, W. Burgess of the White House butchers kindly gave large weights of meat, Mr Scott the police superintendent donated £5, and Walter Lawson of Wallaw Pictures Ltd gave £6 for puddings. Each child was presented with a toy and an orange. The ballroom was provided free of charge by Mr Alf Shepherd the proprietor.

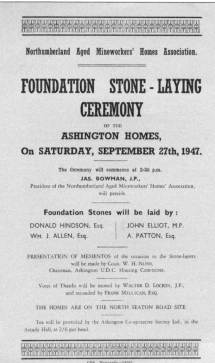

FOUNDATION STONE - LAYING CEREMONY

OF THE

ASHINGTON HOMES,

On SATURDAY, SEPTEMBER 27th, 1947.

The Ceremony will commence at 2-30 p.m.

JAS. BOWMAN, J.P.,

President of the Northumberland Aged Mineworkers' Association, will preside.

Foundation Stones will be laid by :

| DONALD HINDSON, Esq. | JOHN ELLIOT, M.P. |
| WM. J. ALLEN, Esq. | A. PATTON, Esq. |

PRESENTATION OF MEMENTOS of the occasion to the Stone-layers will be made by Coun. W. H. NUNN, Chairman, Ashington U.D.C. Housing Committee.

Votes of Thanks will be moved by WALTER D. LOCKEY, J.P., and seconded by FRANK MILLICAN, ESQ.

THE HOMES ARE ON THE NORTH SEATON ROAD SITE.

Tea will be provided by the Ashington Co-operative Society Ltd., in the Arcade Hall, at 2/6 per head.

CPS., Newcastle—24265

Above: Couple in Aged Miners' Home, *c.* 1950. The idea of providing retirement homes for elderly pitmen and their wives came originally from the Miners' Union. It was thought that if a man had spent most of his life down a coal mine then he deserved a little comfort in his old age. Edward and Agnes Hunter are seen enjoying their cosy cottage where everything revolved around a glowing coal fire.

Left: Programme for the official opening of Bowman Square Aged Miners' Homes, 1948. Each time a new set of homes was opened the organisers had a good excuse to have a party. James Bowman, after whom these homes were named, was a miner and local Union spokesman who ended up with a knighthood and title of Chairman of the National Coal Board. Refreshments were served later that afternoon at the Co-op's Arcade Café.

Ashington Hospital, *c.* 1916. When the mines were first opened up in Ashington, the sick and injured miners and their families were being cared for by the Ashington Nursing Association. The nurses quickly realised the necessity of hospital accommodation for what was fast becoming a very populated area. At the Association AGM in February 1913 the secretary John Craigs JP announced that the various workmen's unions had unanimously agreed to a one penny levy amongst their members for the building fund, and that the buildings would commence at once. Mr George Beaty, Surveyor of Ashington Council, was appointed architect with instructions to design a building with accommodation for twenty-four patients. The hospital was completed in November 1915 and, by a coincidence, the Military Authorities at that time were anxious to have further hospital accommodation for the garrison troops on the east coast of Northumberland. The Nursing Association was approached on behalf of the Local Aid Detachments with a view to the use of the hospital for military purposes, and they patriotically offered Ashington Hospital free of all charges.

Hospital's horse-drawn ambulance, *c.* 1916. Men seen in pseudo-uniform were soldier patients. The building, then in effect a military hospital, was staffed by members of the British Red Cross and military personnel. In 1922 it reverted to its intended purpose as a civilian hospital under a management committee, comprising for the most part officials and employees of the Ashington Coal Company who jointly provided about ninety per cent of its voluntary income.

Hospital's first mechanical ambulance, 1923. Body work was completed by Hallowell Brothers of Ellington. The first addition to the hospital was the War Memorial Ward of twelve beds opened on 9 November 1924, bringing the bed complement to forty-two. The War Memorial itself, consisting of four plaques containing the names of men who had fallen in the First World War, was placed on the wall at the entrance to this ward.

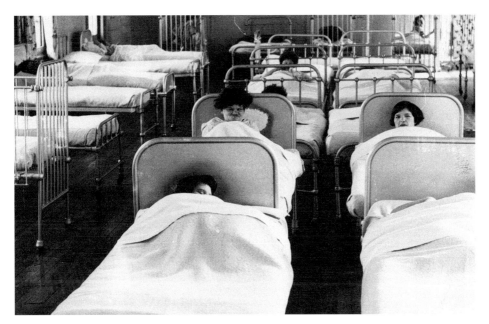

Children in Pity Me Isolation Hospital, around the 1930s. In a 1927 medical report from the regional Medical Officer, Dr Bruce, it was stated: 'Because of the (1926) Miners' Strike, lack of food and adequate sanitation has begun to take its toll. Smallpox is on the increase. Six of the twenty-two cases reported this year come from the same family. I propose that, as a precautionary measure, we open a male/female discharge room, bathing accommodation and a hot-water system at the Isolation Hospital at Pity Me, North Seaton, at a cost of £800.'

Hospital carnival members, 1927. Self-help came from the miners that year who arranged a carnival with all proceeds going into hospital funds. In a report to the governors of Ashington Hospital on 26 February 1927, John Joseph Hall, colliery agent, said: 'The hospital has suffered a severe setback this year owing to the industrial crisis through which we have passed. The building programme has had to be postponed indefinitely.'

SCHEDULE No. 1—WORKMEN'S CONTRIBUTIONS, 1948.

	£	s.	d.
Ashington, Linton, Woodhorn, Ellington, and Lynemouth Mine-workers, Officials, Deputies, Enginemen, and Firemen; Drainers and Estate Workers	5660	0	6
National Coal Board Farm Employees	87	16	8
North Seaton Workmen	42	0	0
Ashington Industrial Co-operative Society Ltd. Employees	150	0	0
Ashington Urban District Council Employees	105	2	4
Ashington Fire and Rescue Station Employees	4	15	0
The United Automobile Association Employees	81	10	0
The British Railways (Ashington Station) Employees	13	8	0
Ashington and District Schoolmasters' Association	6	1	4
Liverpool Victoria Friendly Society Employees	4	4	0
The North-Eastern Electricity Board Employees	20	0	6
The Wallaw Pictures Co. Employees	32	0	8
Ashington Post Office Employees	13	9	11
The Ideal Stores Employees	7	10	0
Mr. John Main's Employees	5	9	4
Mr. J. W. Pearson's Employees	16	14	8
Messrs. Wood Bros. Employees	1	14	3
Messrs. Brough's Employees	5	5	9
Mr. J. Donkin's Employees	6	17	8
Messrs. Shepherd's Employees	5	4	0
The Laburnam Stores Employees	5	19	6
Messrs. Doggart's Employees	4	13	4
Messrs. R. W. Mackenzie's Employees	12	16	4
The Prudential Assurance Co. Employees	10	9	4
Mr. V. G. Stimpson's Employees	15	3	4
Messrs. G. Arrowsmith's Employees	4	9	4
Ashington Food Office Employees	4	11	0
Ashington Police	10	8	0
Mr. Anderson's (Drapers) Employees	1	5	0
Messrs. Snow's Employees	1	13	0
Messrs. Reyrolle's Employees	100	0	0
Ashington Joint Welfare Committee Employees	56	5	4
The Pearl Assurance Co. Employees	3	9	4
Messrs. Carrick's Employees	4	4	6
Messrs. Leech & Co. Employees	7	18	0
Messrs. Derek Crouch's Employees	77	6	6
Mr. W. Todd's Employees	1	10	0
Messrs. W. T. Avery's Employees	0	13	0
The Newcastle Savings Bank Employees	3	19	6
National Union of Mineworkers (Clerical and Supervisory Grades) Employees	310	0	0
Messrs. Colpitt's Factory Employees	146	11	6
Bedlington and District Luxury Coaches Co. Employees	8	18	0
Messrs. Storey & Johnson's Employees	7	9	2
Messrs. Rickard & Baxter's Employees	3	15	6
	£7,072	13	1

Hospital source of income, 1948. This list of subscribers to hospital funds in 1948 shows the benevolence of many well-known shopkeepers and businesses trading at the time.

Ashington Young Mothers' Club, *c.* 1954. A NHS clinic was started in back Station Road for mothers and babies in 1949. These ladies include, from back left: Joyce Todd, Jessie Langdown, Elisabeth Jeffrey, Ann Barton, Dorothy Robertson, Betty Hook, Betty Chapman, Joan Middlemiss, Bell Keach, Sheila Andrew, Sylvia Lewins, Dorothy Richardson, Kitty Ellison, Edna Musk, Ella Locker, Gladys Rowntree, Margaret McMurdo, Mary Rutter, Alice Henderson, Jessie and Mary Patterson, Mrs Weldon, Mrs Taylor, Betty McAlister, Jean Fannon, Dot Jackson, Mary Thompson, Alice Clough, Hazel Cook and Betty Algar.

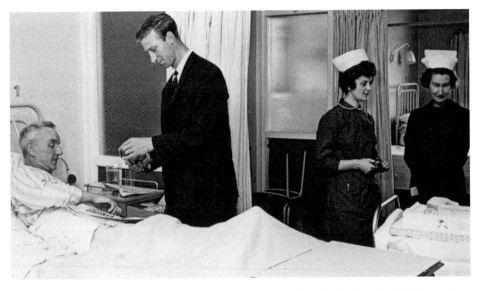

Jack Charlton at Ashington Hospital, August 1966. It was a big day for brothers Bobby and Jack Charlton when they were given a civic reception on the occasion of being part of England's winning World Cup team. Here Jack shows the gold watch he had been given to a patient while Sister Sheila Pattison and Matron Olive Tanner admire a cake iced to replicate Wembley Stadium.

Patients transfer to Wansbeck Hospital, June 1993. The foundation stone for the new Wansbeck Hospital had been laid by Kenneth Clarke, Secretary of State for Health, in March 1990. Here we see the first patients arriving at Wansbeck on the closure of Ashington Hospital, which was demolished during the months of May to August 2004.

Princess Alexandra opens new Wansbeck Hospital, 1993. A brochure commemorating ninety years of Ashington Hospital said: 'Ashington Hospital is now too old and inflexible to offer the modern health services that patients expect, and that can be better provided at the purpose-built Wansbeck General Hospital.'

five

People and Places

Railway bridge, c. 1930. Built initially of wood in the 1850s, this was the only crossing at this part of the River Wansbeck until 1 June 1908, when a sale of land took place concerning Low Black Close for an approach road and bridge, plus proportions of coal remaining un-worked under these lands. Cost of the new road bridge and land was estimated at £12,000. The Duke of Portland donated land on the Ashington side while Lord Barrington reciprocated on the Stakeford side.

Hirst South School. The 'South' saw its first intake of pupils on 12 October 1908. Always alert to what was happening in the village, an entry in the school log for 22 May 1911 reveals that 'School closed this afternoon as a circus is visiting the town.' A stark revelation in the log during the First World War states that on 25 January 1918: 'A very poor attendance again because of the necessity for children to seek and stand waiting for food supplies.'

Vic Hindmarsh marathon dancer, 1925. It was a mania that swept America and finally came to Ashington's Harmonic Hall on 14 June 1925 when the manager at the Harmonic, Vic Hindmarsh, challenged all comers to a 100-hour dance. His accompanist, Tom Swan of Newbiggin, musical director at the Princess Ballroom, also claimed a world piano-playing record. A worn-out-looking Vic is seen resting in the backyard at Hawthorn Road with his dancing partner and two young daughters.

Wyn Gladwin adult dancers, 1993. From back left: Jean Wright, Jean Bush, Julie Brown, Norma Rutter, Brenda Chapman, Helene Henderson, Joan Hydes. Front row: Joyce Cook, Elaine Brooks, Joy Warne, Pat Mason, Marlene Anderson and Frances Skinner.

Ashington Men's Hockey Team, *c*. 1924. Matt Clough, bottom left, was one of the team's leading goal-scorers at the time. Others included Ben Tinkler, Arthur Robertson and Johnnie Graham (all three selected to represent the county), T. Ledgerwood, Len Finlay, Ed Gladson (later played at county level), Joe Ward, John Stoker, George and Ed Tapson, Johnnie Adamson, Hanley, L. Paul, C.B. Pickering, Gould and Evans. All-round sportsman Joe Curry (seated third right) was another great hockey player from that era.

Ashington Ladies' Netball Team, 1950. The team was inaugurated in 1947 and is seen here at Hirst Park School. From left to right, back row: Margaret Elliott, Isobel Reed, Grace Air, Jenny Pratt, Margaret Ridley. Middle row: Dorothy Laws, Frances Rhodes, Jean Porritt, Olive Dent, Bertha Lewis, Joyce Ellis, Jean Hindhaugh. Front row: Mary Willis, Rose Hetherington, Joan Barnes, Irene Copeland, Peggy Neary, Betty Hetherington and Betty Shepherd.

Plane crash at Fifth Row. Ashington did not get through the Second World War unscathed. Disaster struck on 6 June 1940 when a Beaufort Bomber of 22 Squadron Coastal Command misjudged its exact location and plunged into four houses in the Fifth Row, the engine demolishing the downstairs of No. 77, killing both of the Cox parents and seriously injuring daughter Gladys who died the next day. Son Billy Cox survived, but suffered serious burns to one arm.

Ashington's Special Constables, c. 1944. Many prominent figures of the community volunteered to help the regular police force maintain law and order. The centre row includes John William Lillico a colliery blacksmith, Mr Lawrence a Co-op manager, Mr W. Burgess and Mr O. Blevins of the White Shop Butchers, Mr Lillico of Rington's Tea, Mr Hall of the 50/- Tailors. Front row includes Mr R. Mackenzie a painter, J.W. Gibson who owned Gibson's Garage, Will Cookson a Coal Company official, and Inspector Taylor and Sergeant Neilson of the Ashington Police force.

Ashington Girls Training Corps, *c.* 1944. Set up during the Second World War, these Ashington girls helped the war effort by adopting a ship and then knitting socks for the crew as well as becoming pen pals. From left to right, front row: M. Renwick, D. Hindhaugh, Vera McLean, -?-, Mrs Fred Booth, Miss Joisce, Miss Marshall, Margaret Taylor (the police inspector's daughter), Ruby Fotheringham, Elsie Prior, Freda Campbell. Second front row: Betty Tomlinson, -?-, Maureen Main, Doreen Robertson, Vi Randall, Audrey Cairns, Gwen Randall, -?-, Betty Rutherford, M. Algar. Second back row: Eileen Cairns, J. Cairns, Evelyn Skee, E. Pratt, Freda Saltmarsh, Jean Irwin, Mona Langan, Winnie Little, -?-, -?-, Doris Burns, Nancy Johnson. Back row: Katy Mitchell, Elsie Gordon, Joyce Moore, -?-, Jean Nee, Elsie Thomas, Grace Gray, -?-, -?-, E. Scott and Sybil Wardle.

Hirst Park Boys, 1950. There was a special lad in this photograph, although neither he nor his mates knew it at the time. Lanky Jack Charlton, fourth left on the middle row, together with his talented brother Bobby, went on to create a record in 1966 by being the only pair of brothers to be in a football World Cup-winning team.

ASHINGTON HORTICULTURAL SOCIETY'S
ANNUAL FLOWER SHOW AND SPORTS

£30 BRASS BAND CONTEST

will be held on Saturday, August 10th, 1946,

in connection with the above.

TEST PIECE:

FANTASIA'S OWN CHOICE

(Time limit 11 minutes)

Prizes: 1st £12, 2nd £7, 3rd £4, 4th £2.

March Contest on the Stand

(OWN CHOICE). Prizes: 1st Prize £3, 2nd Prize £2.

AN EFFICIENT ADJUDICATOR HAS BEEN ENGAGED

ENTRANCE FEE 10/6 PER BAND

CONDITIONS OF CONTEST:

Bands MUST BE MEMBERS of Northumberland or Durham Association, and all players MUST BE A MEMBER of an Association Band. Entries close on Saturday, Aug. 3rd, 1946.

Draw in the Park at 2-45 p.m. Contest to commence at 3 o'clock

Bands are requested to play up the Street

before the Contest between Grand Hotel and Institute Rd. Entrance to People's Park.

The Committee reserve the right to cancel this contest if insufficient entries received.

Secretaries note the Closing Date of Entries.

Entries to J. Grieve, Secretary,

21, Sixth Row, Ashington

Flower Show Brass Band Contest programme, August 1946. Post-war, the town of Ashington let its hair down and brought back the popular 'Flower Show and Sports'. It was held at People's Park and, as the advertisement says, bands were expected to play 'Up the Street' ... between the Grand Hotel and the Institute Road entrance to the park.

Hirst United, 1947. Scores of local pit lads turned out each Saturday for a game in the
Ashington Welfare League, like this highly successful squad who won the League title and
Booth Cup that same year. From left to right, back row: Jack Dent, Ron Brown, Bobby
Gibson, Harry Graham, Myers Foreman, Tom Morton, Alan Chilton, Bill Ross, Cappy
Graham. Front row: Bernard Jeffries, Gordon Dent, Jackie Grocock, ? Graham, Bobby
Dawson, -?-, Squeak Sanderson and ? Miller.

Ashington FC Squad, 1949. In the seasons 1920-29 the Colliers held a position in the Football
League and played hosts to the likes of Nottingham Forest and Aston Villa in the FA Cup.
During the early 1950s the Colliers had remarkable runs in pursuit of the latter piece of
silverware. This 1949 squad includes Reg Charlton, Ron Brown, Jackie Gallon, Norman West,
Billy Lyons, Ronnie Harrison, Sammy Scott and Gordon Dent. Note the huge crowd.

Ashington Veterans' Team, 1950. Playing against a Pegswood Veteran's team that included the legendary Hughie Gallagher, the Ashington team featured Alex Milburn, father of Wor Jackie. Back row includes Les Common, George Lynch, Jack Swalwell, Bell, Cecil Cochrane, Jim Downie, Bob Wedderburn, Butcher Robson. In front: Jim Thompson, Jacka Turnbull, Alex Milburn, George Thompson and another Thompson. The man in cap, far right, is Bob Thompson, a Back-Overman at Ashington Pit who had been a Sunderland player.

Celebrity Cricket Team, 1952. A remarkable array of sportsmen came together at Pegswood for a charity cricket match. From left to right, back row: Ray King who played for Port Vale and England 'B', Tommy Rigg of Middlesbrough and Ashington, Neville Black of Ashington and Newcastle United, Jackie Milburn of Newcastle and England. Middle row: Jack Watson county cricketer, Ken Prior of Newcastle United, Cyril Brown of Sunderland, Bobby Charlton of Man Utd and England. Front row: Jimmy Scarth of Tottenham, Bobby Gibson was player/manager for Ashington, and George 'Dusty' Down who won the Powderhall Sprint in 1946.

Clement Attlee at Hirst Welfare, 1954. It was a great day for the mining community when Hirst Welfare was chosen to host the All England Schools' Athletic Championships. It proved to be a logistical nightmare to organise the accommodation of 1,800 visiting athletes, but Hirst East headmaster George Hemming organised the games superbly. Seen with Mr Attlee on the perimeter of the running track are Inspector James Macintosh and Richard Percy, Duke of Northumberland.

Ashington & District Motor Club, 1950. Motorcycle scrambling enthusiasts are seen here at Wellhead Dene, Sheepwash, now known as Riverside Park. From left: Ralph Johnson (father of Louis), 'Jopper' Jobson, Louis Johnson, Phillip Middleton, Norman Barker, Colin Stanbury, Ken Massen and Jim Bell.

Ashington Day Continuation School Students, 1923. A brand-new Mining School was later built in Darnley Road, opening in 1930. Pictured from left to right, back row: Tommy Cowan, Arthur Whinnom, Tom Horn, C. Cross, A. Brown. Middle row: William Herod, Jack Summers, J. Hudson, Bill Gibson, G. Dixon, B. Dixon. Front row: Harry Wilson, Bob Thompson, Joe Murray (headmaster), Fred Booth (colliery agent), Bill Davison and George Brownrigg.

Aerial view of Technical College, *c.* 1966. This was an offshoot of the Mining School, and now called Northumberland College. Originally only a three-storey building when opened in the late 1950s, this shows a relatively quiet, neat and tidy view after the last stage had been built.

Ashington Grammar Prefects 1960/61. The school opened quietly on 5 September 1960 with morning prayers conducted by the headmaster in the Assembly Hall. From left to right, back row: Carole Watson, Lorna McNiven, J. Robson, D. Hawkes, R. Bundy, William Wharrier, Barbara Underhill, Pat Hope. Front row: Sylvia Morse, Auriol Taylor (deputy head), Barbara Huggins, Mrs Jean Anderson, George Chapman (headmaster), Leonard Heslegrave (deputy head), John Singer, J.L. Foster and R. Richardson.

Ashington Grammar School staff reunion, 1974. The staff are pictured just before the school's grammar status was replaced by that of comprehensive. From left to right, back row: Richard Houlden (became head at the new Hirst High School), John Wilson (deputy head), Leonard Heslegrave (former deputy head), Bob Cessford (original head of art in 1960, then from 1974 until he retired in 1980, senior master), Michel Duffy (former deputy head who left to take charge at King Edward VI, Morpeth). Front: Miss Hazel Richardson (senior mistress), Gordon Lister (headmaster in 1974), George Chapman (original head) and Mrs Jean Anderson (former senior mistress).

St Aidan's First Communicants, 1951. St Aidan's was the second school to be built in Ashington with the foundation stone being laid by the Lady Mayor of Newcastle on 22 September 1894, accompanied by music from the Ashington Duke Pit Band. Initially, the school was also used as a makeshift church until the Catholic church was built in 1904. Father Connolly, parish priest at St Aidan's RC church, must have renewed his faith in miracles when, on 29 March 1920, the church, the school, priest's house, gardens, cemetery and other lands in the vicinity became the sole property of the Catholic community, all for a bargain price of £337 15s 6d. Catholic numbers in the area were swelled by Irish immigrants, who had come over in the 1850s because of the potato famine, mixed with Italians, pioneered by the likes of young Alfredo Marchetti at the turn of the twentieth century. The Italians established ice cream shops and fish and chip emporiums on practically every corner of town. After the Second World War the local Catholics were further joined by men of Polish extraction. With these young girls, about to make their First Communion, the parish priest seen here far left is Fr Andrew Sheedy who had been an army chaplain during the war. Sadly he died shortly after this photograph was taken. The priest on the right with headmaster John Belshaw is Father Bellamy The two original teachers when the school opened were the Thompson sisters, Margaret Eleanor and Elizabeth Mary who had lived together in Morpeth, but who eventually bought property in September 1921 at Nos 22 and 23 Park Road at a cost of £31 1s for the land.

Ashington Squad for *It's A Knockout*, 20 May 1973. Pitted against near neighbours Blyth at
Hirst Welfare, Ashington came away victorious. Squad members coached by Jim Alder and
Ernie Slaughter (seated third left) included PE teachers Alan Mole and Gwen Woodman with
Sue Green, Eileen Griffiths, Mary Foster, Kathy Thomas, Linda Young, Jackie Armstrong,
Barbara Hudson, Margaret Davies, Bill Lewins, Dave Boon, Mel Robson, Jim Makepeace, Tom
Armstrong, Eric Moore, Don Murray, Ron Morris, Alan Cutter, Dave Skuse, Jack Chisholm,
Paul Slowey, Austin Straker, Jack Watts, Alan Brown and Oliver Cole; arrangements were made
by council official Gerry White, seen in front with beard.

Hirst North School and Bobby Charlton, 1990. It was while playing for Hirst North 'A'
Team in 1948 that young Bobby Charlton was spotted as a potential professional footballer.
He is seen above with pupils after returning to his old school (by then called 'Cavendish and
Milburn First') while promoting his Football School of Excellence for British Gas.

Above: Steve Harmison. Seen relaxing by the swimming pool during the 2004 West Indies tour after taking seven wickets in one innings. Steve, born in October 1978, attended Hirst North then Ashington High School. He is one of the well-known sporting Harmisons whose grandfather Walter played in goal for Hirst East End. Towering well over six feet, Steve started his career with Ashington Cricket Club as a seventeen-year-old.

Right: Kenneth Ferrie. An ex-pupil of Coulson Park First and Hirst High School, former British Boys' Champion, Ken has battled his way up the golf rankings since he took up playing professionally – a far cry from the plastic golf club which he and his brother Iain were given while on holiday as children. As a youth he played at Bedlington Golf Course. The twenty-six-year-old had the distinction of leading the field on the first day of the Open Championship at Troon in 2004.

Left: Jackie Milburn, aged twenty, in 1944. Seen here outside his home in Sixth Row with father Alex, mother Nance and sister Jean. In the early 1950s it was Milburn who kick-started the town of Ashington, putting it well and truly on the map by scoring some of the most spectacular goals ever seen at St James' Park or Wembley Stadium. He endeared himself to the whole of Tyneside, but it was to the people of Ashington that he remained 'Wor Jackie'.

Below: Milburn Cortege leaves Ashington, 12.25 p.m., 13 October 1988. When Jackie Milburn died at the early age of sixty-four, the region lost a great ambassador. This modest son of a pitman personified all that was good in a sportsman. As the cortege left his home in Bothal Terrace just after midday, bound for St Nicholas Cathedral in Newcastle, the streets were lined with local folk, young and old, standing in silence, as seen here crossing Station Bridge.

six

Up The Street

Station Road, *c.* 1890. One of the first shops to open on Station Road in the 1890s, was that of J. Pedelty, a printer, a shop which later became the Portland Printing Works standing on the east side at the entrance down to the railway station. For many years the town's only public telephone was located here.

Station Road and Boer War Memorial, *c.* 1910. This is where the shops petered out to the west and the colliery rows started, although one or two retailers opened up next to the Miners' Theatre in centre. The police station, left, opened in 1897 and the Harmonic Clock – as the Memorial was called – was demolished in the late 1950s.

First World War Victory Arch, 1919. Celebrations and parades for peace were held in July 1919. The first arch was built at the entrance to Station Road beside the newly-built Wallaw Cinema. It was inscribed 'Peace And Honour To Our Brave Heroes'. Thousands of servicemen and women paraded the main street to a service at the Holy Sepulchre where another arch had been erected to celebrate the end of the war.

Blacklock's Department Store, c. 1910. This was the tallest shop in Ashington, towering over other retail establishments and boasting a roof-top café for afternoon tea dances. Built to his own specifications by Newbiggin-man Robert Blacklock, the shop occupied Nos 42-48 Station Road and at the time of this picture, he was in the process of gutting and taking over the two adjacent shops on left.

Station Rd. Ashington.

Above: 'Over the bridge' shopping, *c.* 1920. The stretch of Station Road to the west of the railway became known as 'Middle Market' and one of the workingmen's clubs – the Kicking Cuddy – actually adopted this name. For many years there were more shops and businesses situated here than on the other side of Station Bridge. Music retailers such as Hall and Cardwell, and before that Benny Creigh and Waddington's, were specialists and drew discerning customers through their doors. The town's first banks, such as Lloyds, Martins and the Newcastle Savings Bank were here, together with the Refuge Assurance and later Weatherstone's and Dawson & Sanderson, two of the first travel agents to operate in Ashington. Irishman Paddy Mullen had a high-quality draper's shop here for many years. James Chrisp sold toys as well as newspapers.

Opposite: Doggart's advertisement, *c.* 1930. This is what the youngsters of town were wearing. Winnie Oxnard worked on displays for Blacklocks *and* Doggarts. In 1990 Winnie told the author: 'Robert Blacklock made the shop too posh for Ashington. It wasn't the kind of place miners' wives felt comfortable in. The shop mustn't have been making a profit because Blacklock went into liquidation.'

Advertisement from *Ashington Collieries Magazine*, December 1923. The department store owned by Russell Cook dominated the area around the 'Grand Corner', in fact, when Mr Cook placed this advertisement, he called it 'Cook's Corner'. As can be seen, you could buy anything here for a Christmas present from a tea cosy to a silk macintosh.

Station Road looking east. It was the east side of Station Road that attracted the retail giants such as Woolworth and Boots, recognising the potential that a town of Ashington had with a mushrooming population and the spending power of its mining community. Department stores like Blacklock's (later Doggarts and now Mackay's), Russell Cook's (later Shepherd's now Ethel Austin) and Arrowsmith's (now Bon Marche) gave the main street a touch of class.

W. Forster's music shop, c. 1920. This old shop in Station Road is displaying some of the first phonographs to go on sale. The window sign says that they also sell Edison-Bell records. Mr Forster and his family are seen outside the shop doorway. In that same year, on behalf of Ashington Empire Theatre and Picture Hall Ltd, William Miller of 21 Station Road purchased two large plots of land for £837 in 'Old Lane' which we know now as Lintonville where the 'Shows' or Miller's Amusements were held each year.

British Legion parade, *c.* 1938. Station Road has been ideal for parades throughout the years. Harold Speight snr, then secretary of the British Legion, is on the left with George Holland in the centre as standard bearer on this Remembrance Day parade. The old Miners' Theatre is on the right, this was shortly before the frontage was taken down to build the new Regal Cinema. St Aidan's church and the old police station are on the left.

Band parades past Regal Cinema, *c.* 1970. The band without uniforms has been identified as possibly coming from Hazelrigg Colliery. You can now see the Regal Cinema in all its glory, undoubtedly the most sumptuous picture palace in Ashington, capable of seating over 1,000 patrons. It was especially popular on a Sunday night when the same film was shown at four of the town's cinemas.

Station Road looking west, *c.* 1938. George Arrowsmith (shop on the right) opened up a large department store at No. 2 Portland Buildings. If that location sounds puzzling to present-day shoppers, it later became No. 4 Woodhorn Road. On 5 May 1919, George was able to buy his leasehold outright from the Duke of Portland for £115. He also owned a menswear shop on the other side of the street at No. 26 Station Road for which he paid £57 10s.

Station Road looking east, *c.* 1950. This is a scene that will evoke fond memories, when there was hardly a car to be seen and those that did own one could park outside the shop of their preference. That forlorn bike cast aside on the pavement on the right tells of a bygone era when other people's property was respected and things could be safely left unattended.

Station Road parade, 1953. This wide road was ideal for a parade of floats in the 1950s. It was an era when shops and shopping changed very little. James Chrisp had two shops: the one above at No. 58 and another 'over the bridge'. He was a well-known figure and a member of the Round Table. Alfred Boast's shop sold clothing of a 'sturdy' nature, such as donkey jackets and Army haversacks, ideal for carrying 'bait'.

Parade past The Silver Library, 1953. The photograph was taken from the upstairs of Badiali's ice cream shop. Louis and John Badiali can be seen in the foreground – spot their identical balding heads. Ashington did not possess its own purpose-built public library until the mid-1960s. Books could be borrowed from here for sixpence – a piece of silver!

Above: Buffalo Cinema, *c.* 1955. The Buff was a cosy cinema with 'love-seats' set out in hideaway corners where courting couples could do what courting couples have always done. The Buff closed down in 1967. Badiali's shop can be seen next door (later to become Marchetti's and now Mario's Café). On the far right is one of several butcher's called The White Shop because of their distinctive white exterior. They belonged to the well-respected Burgess family.

Right: Ashington Colliery Band parade, *c.* 1974. The parade is led on the left by band stalwart Ellis Williams, with conductor Maurice Priestly on the right. Ellis had been attached to the band when it was known as the North Seaton Colliery Band. However, in the early 1930s this had been the Ashington Silver Band when playing for the Wesleyan Central Hall Methodists.

Station Road looking east, *c.* 1972. There are a few cars travelling through but a zebra crossing affords safety and peace of mind. The John Collier tailor's shop on the right was once managed by Roly Cairns, father of Janice who became a celebrated opera singer. The retail trade 'up the street' was still thriving and there was not a sign of the now all-pervading charity shops.

Station Road, *c.* 1988. There is more happening now in spite of the rain that brings out the occasional umbrella. One landmark missing at the top of the photograph is the Grand Hotel, replaced by a concrete building that does little to appease those lovers of fine architecture who deplored the Grand's ignominious end in 1973. This part of Station Road was pedestrianized in 1990.

seven

Pit Work

Introduction to pit work, *c.* 1938. The Ashington Coal Company's Training Scheme was one of the first in Britain to recognise that unless young lads were trained in the art of pit work then production could fall and accidents occur. Some hints on blackboard: be punctual, conscientious and reliable … develop skill in modern machine mining … continue your education at the Mining School.

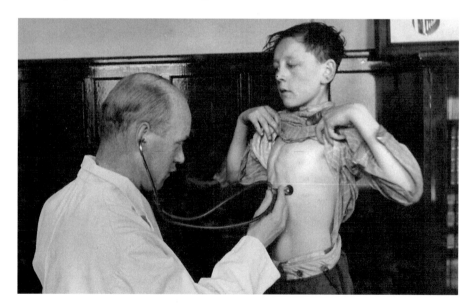

Trainee medical, *c.* 1939. Medical checks at the colliery revealed that many young boys were undernourished. This was considered counter-productive by the ACC and attempts were made to 'fatten them up'. Lads had to work on the screens for a few weeks before getting a place on the sixteen-week scheme. Each trainee was given a set of navy-blue overalls and a pair of gaiters.

Free milk at the pit canteen, *c.* 1936. One way to 'beef-up' the lads was to give them a free gill of milk each morning from the ACC's own dairy farm. Young lads usually went to the colliery where their fathers worked. Although the school-leaving age then had risen to fourteen years, if you could prove that you had a job to go to then the Education Authority allowed boys to leave as early as thirteen.

Lecture time for trainees, *c.* 1938. The man in charge, Joe Dockerty, had been a safety officer before joining the training scheme. Another of the leading lights on the scheme was Mr Charlton, and other trainers in the 1940s included Tommy Templeton, Jack Crook, Wilf Dick and Jack Kirkup.

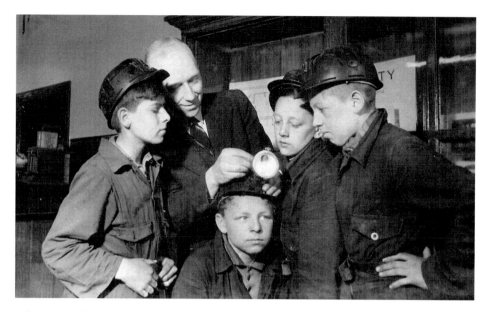

Adjusting cap lamp, *c.* 1938. The miners were not enamoured of the electric lamp because of having to carry the heavy battery needed to provide energy. Occasionally, the battery did not last the seven-hour shift and you ended up in the dark. In the 1930s some of the local mines were still classed as 'Naked Flame' pits where miners were allowed to use carbide lamps to light their way. In spite of the threat of instant dismissal, smoking was still rife down below well into the 1950s.

How to hew the coal, *c.* 1939. This lecture would be something of a futile exercise. The only way to show a lad how to hew a coal was at the face itself. The man swinging the pick seems to have worked a genuine shift underground as he is a bit dusty. It would be a year or two before fourteen-year-olds were allowed to go on to a real coal face and they would be eighteen before starting piecework.

Hewing on the training face, *c.* 1939. This small lad is barely big enough or strong enough to lift the pick, let alone swing it with any venom at the hard coal seam. One-to-one training was rare in the early days of the training scheme. The coal face was usually based in the Plessey Seam of the Duke Pit.

Marching inbye, *c.* 1939. If you were walking towards the coal face you were deemed to be going 'inbye'. Conversely, at the end of the shift you walked 'outbye' to the shaft bottom. It is almost as though these lads are rehearsing for *Snow White and the Ten Dwarfs*.

Above: Coal face pep talk, *c.* 1938. There is something charming about the image of a gnarled pitman passing on hints to lads young enough to be his grandsons. The two apprentice pitmen sit amidst the broken coal and pit props whilst the experienced miner imparts worthwhile gems that will last them a lifetime.

Left: Experience meets youth, *c.* 1939. This young Jack-the-lad trainee swaggers on the corner of the colliery offices where he is met by a towering overman, instantly recognisable by his shiny kneepads and waistcoat.

Waiting in the pit yard, *c.* 1938. Youngsters new to the life were often overawed by the sheer size of Ashington Colliery and its myriad ancillary trades including electricians, plumbers and mechanics. If a young boy was brainy enough then he could opt for one of the trades, but the majority ended up wielding a pick and shovel.

Ashington Colliery lamp cabin, *c.* 1938. The young lads parade outside the lamp cabin waiting for their battery-operated cap lamps. The heavy battery had to be strapped to a belt around the waist. It often leaked acid which irritated, then burned the backside.

Underground lecture, *c.* 1939. It might have seemed boring at the time, but some of the hints passed on by the men in charge were to prove invaluable when the youngsters were faced with a situation they had never previously experienced. One of the first graves dug at the Holy Sepulchre church was for John Johnston, a fourteen-year-old laddie who was killed on his very first day down the Bothal Pit.

Training for haulage, *c.* 1936. The first job a lad had to do down the pit was that of a transit worker. That is, being part of a team of shiftworkers whose main task was to get the tubs of coal out of the pit. 'Hanging on' and 'knocking off' were two phrases ingrained into a boy's vocabulary. The implement on the rope was a 'hambone'.

Above: Rapping the signals, *c.* 1939. The fastest means of communicating down the pit was by a series of bell wires that traversed the main roadways. Each rap of the bell had significance to others in the pit, especially those working on the haulage system. The most important rap was 20; a rap of 20 on the bells signalled the end of the shift, or Lowse, as it was called.

Right: Young trainee, *c.* 1938. This young lad has a scarf around his neck indicating that his place of work was cold. In wintertime it was not unusual for snow to be brought underground on top of trams that had been standing overnight in the timber yard. It seems incredible, but snowball fights did occasionally take place 1,000ft below ground!

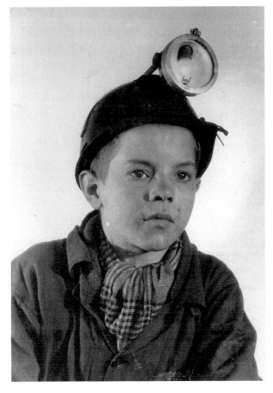

Trainees at lessons, *c.* 1939. A room was set aside in the training centre where lessons could take place about once a week. Subjects taught included mine safety and haulage techniques, as well as the basic principles of electricity.

Joe Dockerty with trainees, *c.* 1938. Mr Dockerty had been appointed as safety officer by the Ashington Coal Company in the early 1920s. Each month he wrote an article on 'Safety in the Mine' which appeared in the monthly Coal Company magazine. It seemed natural that he be appointed training centre manager when the scheme began in the late 1930s.

Wilf Dick gives first aid advice, *c.* 1938. It was he who taught many young lads the ways of administering vital help to stricken colleagues. Accidents down the mine often ended with fatalities – it was a dangerous occupation. The first aider was a vital member of the workforce in treating wounds before a doctor arrived on the scene underground.

Learning about lights, *c.* 1938. Initially, underground workings were illuminated by the dim light of a candle. These were gradually replaced by carbide lamps, then safety lamps (Glennies) and cap lamps, powered by a battery. The use of naked flames in pits was the cause of many disasters when the deadly methane gas was present. A spark was sufficient to set off the most horrendous gas explosions.

Checking roof supports, *c.* 1938. Sometimes, the only thing holding up thousands of tons of strata above a miner's head was a steel plank and a wooden prop. Planks, or straps, were placed at intervals of one yard to ensure safety. In some pits the seams were as low as one foot nine inches. The instructor here is showing the lads the function of a 'headtree': a small block of wood balanced on top of a prop to adjust its height.

Introducing the pit pony, *c.* 1939. Many trainees had never been up close to any animal, let alone a ten-hands high pony. The first job was to learn about the pony's harness and where each item fitted. Each pony was allocated a stall in one of the many stables that housed ponies during their 20-year stay underground.

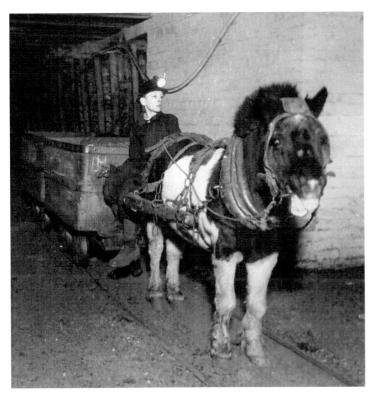

Riding the limmers, c. 1938. The ponies were yoked with wooden shafts called limmers. This enabled them to be hitched to either a tub or a tram that was pulled along a narrow-gauge rail called a rolleyway. Tubs were used to hold about half a ton of coal, while trams could transport wooden props or other material. This pony seems to be having a good laugh about something.

Trainee on underground phone, c. 1938. This was probably the first time this youngster had been on the phone, either on the surface or underground. There were only a few underground telephones placed strategically at the shaft-bottom, coal face or 'flats' where transit men congregated. Miners living in Ashington probably did not have phones in their houses until the 1970s.

Drawing the chocks, c. 1950. It was the job of an experienced Drawer to remove timber and planks once the seam of coal had been filled off and the conveyor belt advanced to its next position. Once a chock was 'released' there was always a chance that the roof might cave in, and that was a signal for the Goaf (surplus roof) to come clattering down – an experience guaranteed to put the fear of God into unsuspecting pit novices. During their shift, the Cuttermen built a series of softwood chocks to support the roof for when it is time for the Drawers to move in and remove the planks which were salvaged, i.e. taken outbye, and straightened in order to be used again. This might have been deemed as false economy, but Ashington Coal Company always instilled into their workers the need to economise and recycle as much as possible. The language of 'Drawing the Chocks' was often used by spectators at a football match to urge their team to 'topple' one of the opposition with cries of: 'Gan on, Geordie, draw his bluddy chocks.'

Waiting in the wages queue, *c.* 1939. The wages department at Ashington Colliery was probably the miners' favourite place, especially on a Friday morning. Trainees were paid according to age and could not get a man's wage until they were twenty-one. Lads in this queue, joined by some mature pitmen, could normally expect to earn about thirty shillings a week.

Pit canaries, *c.* 1950. Pockets of stythe (blackdamp) often went undetected by sight or smell. If there was any suspicion of a lethal gas lurking in an underground roadway, then the deputy responsible for that place collected a canary in its cage from the surface and took it inbye towards the face. At the first sign of the bird's distress, the pit official declared the place unfit. Sadly, this was often too late for the canary.

Above: Collecting a pit tally, *c.* 1950. Each miner was allocated his own tally which would identify him as being underground. Note the board with tallies for those working in the Duke Pit and the Bothal Pit. A joiner named J. Ford (see name chalked on his saw) picks his tally containing the initial letter of his surname and number from the Duke Pit board.

Left: At the deputy's kist, *c.* 1950. The kist (chest) was placed strategically so that it gave maximum access to all the men who worked in this area. The deputy had sole responsibility for everything that happened in his 'flat'. Far right is an overman – you can tell by his hat being on back-to-front. Far left could be the deputy, and the two figures in the centre are either electricians or mechanics; pitmen didn't wear overalls until the 1980s.

Keeping the score, *c*. 1950. Each Ashington pit was split into districts and each seam divided into 'flats' or working places. A target was set to ensure that production was constant or improving from week to week. Here a pit official is chalking on a Carl Pit Bensham district. The 'Aim' was the target and the 'Hit' was what was achieved.

Working the checkweigh, *c*. 1950. Reliable men were appointed by the Miners' Union to check the weight of each tub that came out of the pit. Each filler and putter placed his own token on to the back of the tub which identified them as being responsible for that tub. The man outside the cabin window is shouting out the token number so that the checkweighman can keep a record.

Above: Duke of York at Ashington, 1928. The town is no stranger to royalty and it was the turn of the Duke of York to visit Ashington and its coalmines in 1928. The Duke was later to become King George VI when his brother Edward VIII abdicated. He is seen front right on the steps leading from Ashington Screens accompanied by coal company officials.

Left: Anthony Eden at Lynemouth Pit, *c.* 1953. The colliery had just undergone a huge re-development programme, necessitating a new building for No. 2 shaft. Prime Minister Eden stands with engineer Cecil Bewick before going underground. In 1966, Bewick's Drift helped solve Lynemouth Colliery's problems following a disastrous underground fire.

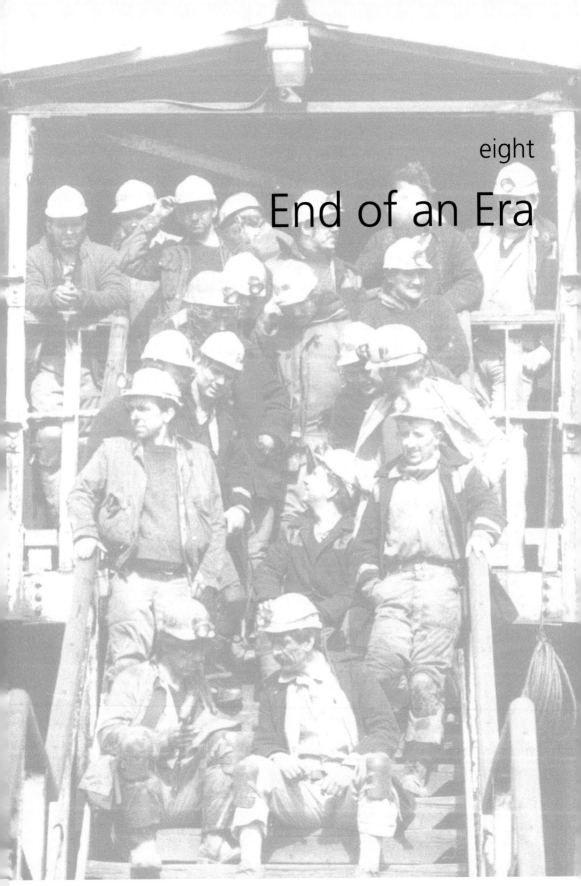

eight

End of an Era

'High' Ashington aerial view looking west, *c.* 1973. At the top, the Second, Third, Fourth, Fifth and Sixth Rows had already been superseded by the new housing estate of Northumberland Close etc. This then was the changing face of the top end of Ashington. Portland Park is in foreground with Ashington YMCA.

Right: Hippodrome Theatre closes, 1960. This was the first of Ashington's five cinemas to close when bingo fever struck and it was taken over by showman Jack Richardson. The Hipp, as it was known, had a change of programme three times a week, showing feature films that had been seen earlier at the Regal, Buffalo and Wallaw.

Below: Ashington Railway Station, January 1964. The town's railway system fell under Dr Beeching's axe in 1963. It had not been used by enough passengers to make it viable. The station was demolished along with Tweedy's coal depot (seen far left), making way for Wansbeck Square with its council office accommodation and Amos Hinton's, the town's first purpose-built supermarket.

Priestman's Institute, 1979. By then it was standing empty, victim of the Ashington miners' fickle social habits. Not enough men were playing billiards and snooker so it was closed. The last secretary was Billy Staines. Some of the popular caretakers in the 1950s and '60s included the left-handed billiard player Bill Shell, the slow-talking Wilson Graham and ex-RAF boxer Sammy Morgan.

Second Block, Maple Street, c. 1960. Among the first of Hirst's colliery rows to be built around 1900 at a cost of about £90 per house, the back doors of Maple opened straight out into the lane with its outdoor toilets and bin corners that spewed dust all over when the binmen made their weekly call.

Woodhorn church, *c.* 1973. St Mary's Woodhorn became a cultural centre and museum for travelling art in the mid-1970s. It is seen here as the backdrop for an annual six-mile race that took place on a circular route from Newbiggin to Ashington and back. The museum fell victim to council economies in the late 1990s and closed completely.

Woodhorn Miners' Union Officials picketing in London, 1980. By the time this delegation travelled down to protest in London, the fate of Woodhorn Colliery was already sealed. It was to close in February 1981. Men from left include Barry Furness, Les Rowntree, Peter Waddell, Bill Scott, Tommy Todd, Sammy Scott, Alec Wallace, Joe Smith, Gordon Boak, Norman Clough, Jack White, Jack Wren and Larry Taylor.

COAL-ITION

The new smelter for Alcan Aluminium will need energy, the source of which will be the coal from nearby Lynemouth Colliery.

Alcan looks forward to a long and mutually prosperous relationship with the men of Lynemouth... and the National Coal Board in general.

ALCAN
Aluminium in action

Above: Last of the sea-coalers, 2003. This is a trade that has been going on as long as waste coal has been tipped into the sea. But now Joe 'Georgia' Smith finds it difficult to fill sufficient bags of coal washed up on the beach to make a living. In the distance is Alcan Power Station which runs three generators: two for the National Grid and one to supply its own energy.

Left: Ashington Post advertisement, 1968. When the Canadian firm of Alcan Aluminium chose Lynemouth as a site rather than one in Wales they were greeted with open arms. Alcan was thought to be the forerunner of the new industries that were to be lured into the area to replace an ageing King Coal. Whenever Ellington Colliery has been threatened with closure it has been their friendly customers at Alcan who have pledged support.

Above: Striking Miners at Ashington Central Workshops, November 1984. Here we have the sad sight of a confrontation between the police and picketing miners. Linda Stevenson was working as a reporter for a local newspaper when she covered this story. After Ashington Pit closed in 1988, the Area Workshops continued to provide mechanical back-up to collieries all around the UK until closing in the 1990s.

Right: Ellington Colliery, February 1985. The year-long miners' strike is all but over. What began as a trickle back to work becomes a deluge as miners realise that winning the battle is not an option. The strike signalled the rundown of mining in the North East.

Ashington last miners on Heapstead, March 1988. The end had been predicted as far back as 1960 when the cost of coal produced far outweighed its selling price. But it was coal that gave birth to Ashington, and if it had not been for those black diamonds then so many things would not have taken place here – no emerging communities, no records of achievement or strife, success and failure.

The last shift, March 1988. The walk from pithead to the baths seemed longer than usual for these men emerging from their last day underground. Many hands were wrung in despair on that fateful day. 'The town is doomed', or so it was reckoned. Yet, here we are, almost twenty years later, and there is no obvious sign of its demise.

Cambois Power Station chimneys, *c.* 1980. Built in 1959, the power station at Cambois symbolised security to the nearby coalmining community of Ashington, providing an extra, guaranteed market for coal from the region's pits and, as such, was welcomed with open arms. No thoughts then of polluting the atmosphere as its four massive chimneys belched smoke into the atmosphere. The chimneys were demolished in February 2004.

Other local titles published by The History Press

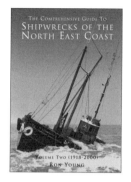

Shipwrecks of the North East Coast Volume Two (1918 – 2000)
RON YOUNG

In this second volume, from the last years of the Second World War, to the end of the twentieth century, Ron Young charts the history of the ships, boats, submarines and their crews, that were lost along the north-east coast from Berwick-on-Tweed to Whitby, and the brave lifeboat crews that went to their aid, whatever the danger to themselves. This comprehensive guide is an absorbing companion volume to *Shipwrecks of the North East Coast – Volume One (1740 – 1917)*
0 7524 1750 9

Blyth Volume II
BOB BALMER AND GORDON SMITH

Although the port of Blyth dates back to the twelfth century, the town originated in the early eighteenth century. Industries such as coal mining, fishing, shipbuilding and, at one time, the salt trade, played a large part in the development of the Northumberland town and this book of over 200 archive images examines their role in Blyth's past and present.
07524 3349 0

Northumberland The Power of Place
STAN BECKENSALL

This book shows the outstanding natural beauty, distinctive geology and rich archaeology of this county. Famous sites that delight visitors – Berwick, Holy Island, Hadrian's Wall and the Cheviots – are featured alongside lesser known places such as Old Berwick, Edlington, Ford and Etal. When layers of time are peeled from these special places, the result is a microcosm of the county, captured in prose and poetry, photographs from the air and ground, and paintings and drawings
07524 1907 2

Prehistoric Northumberland
STAN BECKENSALL

For this book, Stan Beckensall's study area lies largely to the north of Hadrian's Wall, which cuts a swathe across much older sites. His account looks at how landscape was used since hunter-gatherers roamed the wilderness, through the great changes brought about by farming, the erection of monuments, burials, settlements and defences. He explains how tools, weapons, pottery and jewellery help build a picture of life in prehistoric Northumberland.
07524 2543 9

If you are interested in purchasing other books published by The History Press, or in case you have difficulty finding any of our books in your local bookshop, you can also place orders directly through our website
www.thehistorypress.co.uk